AFRICAN HISTORICAL DICTIONARIES
Edited by Jon Woronoff

Historical Dictionary
of
THE GAMBIA

2nd edition

by
HARRY A. GAILEY

African Historical Dictionaries, No. 4

The Scarecrow Press, Inc.
Metuchen, N.J., & London
1987

Library of Congress Cataloging-in-Publication Data

Gailey, Harry A.
    Historical dictionary of the Gambia.

    (African historical dictionaries ; no. 4)
    Bibliography: p.
    1. Gambia--History--Dictionaries. I. Title.
II. Series.
DT509.5.G34 1987   966'.51'00321   87-9897
ISBN 0-8108-2001-3

For

L. A. B. and L. E. B.

with gratitude for R. J. B.

CONTENTS

FOREWORD

A narrow sliver of land along the river that gives it sustenance, the Gambia is manifestly one of the most artificial states in Africa. It was demarcated by rival colonial powers and ruled by Great Britain until independence in 1965. Given its small size and population, scarce natural resources, and modest economic potential, it was assumed that the country could not survive long. Yet, despite a confederation with Senegal, which virtually surrounds it, the Gambia has managed to go its own way for over two decades.

The country's survival surprised observers no less than the fact that the Gambia also managed to steer a relatively successful course on many other fronts. It maintained democracy in a multiparty state with free elections. It overcame various economic crises, many of them the fault of world markets or climatic conditions. And it created a national spirit among the disparate components of society. How this was done, and by whom, is recounted in this revised edition, which brings up-to-date a story that is traced back many centuries.

We are pleased that the Historical Dictionary of the Gambia could be revised by the author of the original edition, Harry A. Gailey. Professor Gailey, who teaches history and is the Coordinator of African Studies at San Jose State University, is one of the leading authorities on the country. He has written A History of the Gambia, which is used in the school system there, as well as nine books and numerous articles and essays focusing on West Africa. In addition to being informative, his work is concise and readable, an ideal introduction to a very interesting place.

Jon Woronoff
Series Editor

ABBREVIATIONS

CD&W	Colonial Development and Welfare
CDC	Colonial Development Corporation
DCA	Democratic Congress Alliance
DP	Democratic Party
GNP	Gambia National Party
GNU	Gambia National Union
GWU	Gambia Workers Union
GOMB	Groundnut Oilseeds Marketing Board
MCP	Muslim Congress Party
PPA	People's Progressive Alliance
PPP	People's Progressive Party (originally Protectorate People's Party)
RAC	Royal African Corps
UP	United Party
WAFF	West Africa Field Force

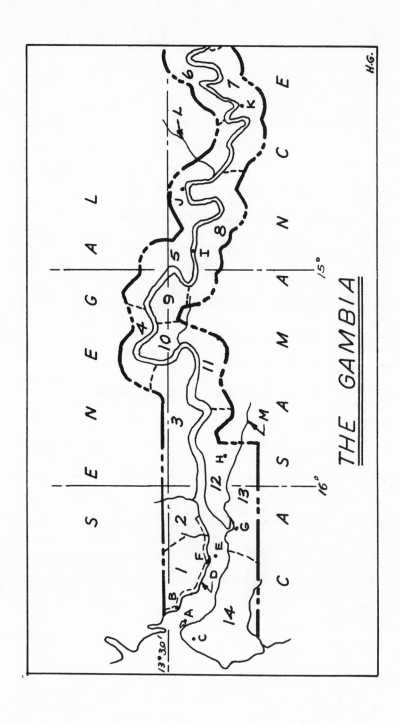

THE GAMBIA

MAP KEY

Nineteenth Century States

1. Niumi
2. Jokadu
3. Baddibu
4. Saloum
5. Niani
6. Wuli
7. Tomani

8. Jimara
9. Eropina
10. Niamina
11. Jarra
12. Kiang
13. Foni
14. Kombo

Towns and Other Sites

A. St. Marys Island, &
    Banjul (Bathurst)
B. Ft. Bullen
C. Sukuta (Sabaji)
D. The Ceded Mile
E. James Island
F. Albreda
G. Bentang

H. Sankandi
I. MacCarthy Island &
    Georgetown
J. Karantaba (Pisania)
K. Basse
L. Sami Creek (Bolon)
M. Bintang Creek

CHRONOLOGY OF IMPORTANT EVENTS

13th Century. Possible date of construction of stone circles by either Jola or Mandingo people. First southeastward migrations of significant numbers of Fulbe probably took place during this time.

13th to 15th Centuries. Period of Malian hegemony over the western Sudan. Gambian Mandingo kingdoms were the westernmost extension of that empire. Large numbers of Muslim converts appeared in the Senegambia.

16th to 17th Centuries. Period of state building among the Wolof in Senegal. Development of Jolof, Walo, Baol, and Cayor. Serer kingdoms of Sine and Saloum also developed in this period. First permanent European settlements in Senegambia during this time. Gradual acceleration of the slave trade.

18th Century. Creation of Islamic theocracy in the Futa Toro and continued conversion of large numbers of Gambians, particularly Fulbe, to Islam. Century-long French-British conflicts in Senegambia which disrupted trade and helped keep the slave trade to a minimal level.

1455 and 1456. First two Portuguese voyages (Cadamosto and Usidimare) to the Gambia River.

1458. Diego Gomez explored the Gambia River.

1553. First English voyages to the Gambia.

1588. First English monopoly company for West African trade.

1620. Richard Jobson, trade factor, sent to the Gambia.

1621. Dutch West Indies Company established at Goree.

1651. Courlanders in the Gambia; built fort on St. Andrews (James) Island. Commonwealth Guinea Company formed.

1652. Prince Rupert in the Gambia.

1660. Royal Adventurers Company formed.

1661. English captured James Island on March 19.

1668. Gambia Adventurers Company established.

1672. French Senegal Company formed.

1677. French captured Goree.

1681. French established Albreda.

1684-1750. Royal African Company.

1689-1783. Trade wars in Senegambia between France and Great Britain.

1696. French Royal Senegal Company established.

1730. Francis Moore, factor for Royal African Company, present in the Gambia.

1750. Company of Merchants Trading in Africa formed.

1758. French bases in Senegal captured.

1765-1783. British Province of the Senegambia.

1779. James Fort destroyed for last time.

1783-1820. Gambia again controlled by Company of Merchants.

1790. Major Houghton left the Gambia for Timbuktu.

1795-1798. Mungo Park's explorations from the Gambia.

1805. Beginning of Mungo Park's second expedition.

1808. British abolition of the slave trade.

1816. Purchase of St. Mary's Island from King of Kombo and beginnings of Bathurst (Banjul).

1821. Gambia placed under jurisdiction of Sierra Leone.

1823. First British establishment in April at MacCarthy Island. Arrival of first contingent of Christian missionaries.

1826. The King of Barra granted the Ceded Mile to Great Britain.

1827-1831. The Barra War between the British and the King of Barra.

1830. First recorded shipment of peanuts from the Gambia.

1843. Gambia created a separate Colony with Executive and Legislative Councils.

1851. Beginnings of Soninke-Marabout Wars in Kombo.

1853. The King of Kombo ceded a portion of Kombo to the British.

1855. Marabout attack upon British Kombo and Bathurst.

1857. French surrender Albreda.

1860-1867. Ma Bâ attempted to create a Senegambia Islamic empire.

1861-1881. Alfa and Musa Molloh created the Fulbe state of Fuladu.

1862. Marabouts invade Barra.

1864. Amer Faal's operations in Niumi. Fodi Kabba attacked Yundum.

1865. Report of Parliamentary Committee on West Africa.

1866. Gambia became a part of British West African Settlements once again.

1866-1870. First negotiations for exchange of the Gambia between Great Britain and France.

1873-1875. Fodi Silla destroys remaining Soninke power in Kombo.

1875-1876. Second period of negotiations for exchange of the Gambia between Great Britain and France.

1877-1887. Civil war in Baddibu between forces of Bairam Cisse, Saër Maty, and Mamadou N'Dare.

1888. Gambia became a separate colony; reinstatement of Legislative and Executive Councils.

1889. Anglo-French agreement which fixed the present boundaries of the Gambia.

1891. International Boundary Commission sent to Gambia.

1892. Fodi Kabba attacked Boundary Commission and was driven into the Casamance.

1894. Fodi Silla captured by the French and exiled. First comprehensive Ordinance for governing the Protectorate.

1900. Travelling Commissioner Sitwell's party ambushed at Sankandi.

1901. British-French punitive expedition and death of Fodi Kabba. Office of Administrator upgraded to Governor.

1904. Anglo-French Convention began the Entente and granted to the French the right for a mid-river port.

1913. General revision of Ordinance for the governing of the Protectorate.

1914-1918. First World War. Gambia Company of WAFF saw service in the Cameroon and East Africa.

1915. Enlargement of Legislative Council.

1919-1922. Redemption of French five franc piece.

1923. Opening of Armitage School, Georgetown.

1928. Bathurst Trade Union formed.

1931. Urban District Council created in Bathurst.

1932. Bathurst African nominated member appointed to Legislative Council.

1933. General reorganization of Protectorate government and courts system.

1935. Name of Urban District Council changed to Bathurst Town Council.

1939-1945. World War II. Gambian troops of WAFF active in China-Burma-India theater. Yundum airbase constructed for use by Allied ferry services.

1940. First British Colonial Development and Welfare Act.

1943. K. W. Blackburne's report on immediate and long-range economic needs of the Gambia.

1945-1950. Reconstruction of port, street, and sewer facilities of Bathurst (Banjul) with Colonial Development and Welfare funds.

1946. Reorganization and enlargement of Legislative Council.

1948-1951. Yundum egg fiasco.

1949-1952. Wallikunda rice scheme.

1951. New Constitution. Reorganization of Legislative Council which provided for two elected members from Bathurst. Democratic Party (DP) formed.

1952. Muslim Congress Party (MCP) formed. United Party (UP) formed. First class at Yundum College for teachers.

1953. Victoria Hospital opened in Bathurst (Banjul). Meeting of 34 Gambian representatives to revise Constitution.

1954. New Constitution allowing direct elective principle for seven members of the Legislative Council.

1957. Sinking of Barra ferry in May with loss of over 50 lives.

1959. Gambia Workers Union created. Protectorate People's Party formed; later called People's Progressive Party (PPP).

1960. New Constitution; 34-member House of Representatives. Democratic Congress Alliance (DCA) created.

1961. P. S. N'Jie became the first Gambian Chief Minister.

1962. New Constitution allowing full internal self government and a 36-member House of Representatives with ministerial government. D. K. Jawara became Prime Minister.

1963. First major comprehensive census of the Gambia.

1965. Voters reject proposal for a Republic. The Gambia achieved independence from Great Britain on February 18.

1970. Voters approved proposals for a Republic in April. Sir Dauda Jawara became the first President of the Gambia.

1972. Elections. United Party elected only 3 members to 28 for PPP in House of Representatives. President Jawara reelected President.

1975-79. First Sahel drought period.

1976. Formation of National Convention Party (NCP).

1977. Elections for House of Representatives and President. PPP won almost 70% of popular vote, 28 seats in House, and Sir Dauda was reelected President.

1981. Attempted coup d'etat in July in Banjul by disaffected political opponents of PPP government. Intervention by Senegalese military restored order and President Jawara. Over 600 killed in Banjul and vicinity. Uprising led to creation of Confederation of Senegambia in December.

1982. Elections for House of Representatives and President. PPP won 27 seats to 3 for NCP. Sir Dauda reelected President with 72.5% of popular vote.

1986. Formation of Gambia Peoples Party (GPP).

CONSTITUTIONAL ADVANCE SINCE 1938: A CHART

Year	Legislature		Elective Council or Ministry	
	Official Membership	Unofficial Membership	Official Membership	Unofficial Membership
1938	Governor + 6	4 (1 representing Muslim interests, 1 repr. commercial int., 2 repr. African int.)	Governor + 4	None
1947	Governor + 3 ex-officio + 3 nominated	7 (including 1 elected & 4 repr. Protect.)	Governor + 5	3 (2 nominated unofficials from Legislative Council and elected member)
1952[a]	Governor + 3 ex-officio + 4 nominated	8 (3 elected, 4 nominated to repr. the Divisions of Protectorate, 1 repr. commerce)	Governor + 6	4 (3 elected members of Legislative Council and 1 nominated, of whom 2 were appointed members of the Government without Portfolio)
1954[b]	Governor + 4 ex-officoi (incl. Senior Commissioner + 1 Gambian Public Officer)	16 (4 directly elected by Colony 7 directly elected by Protec. 3 elected by these 11 1 nominated to rep. commerce 1 other nominated)	Governor + 5 (as for Leg. Council)	7 (of whom 3 have been appointed Ministers)
1960[c]	4 ex-officio 3 nominated	27 (7 directly elected by Colony 12 directly elected by Protect. 8 chosen by Protect. chiefs)	Governor + 4	6 (4 Ministers directly responsible for government departments)
1962		36 (7 directly elected by Colony 25 directly elected by Protect. 4 chosen by Protect. chiefs)		8 Ministers of a Responsible Government under direction of Chief Minister

[a] Vice President appointed; [b] Speaker to be appointed by the Governor; [c] Name of Legislature changed to House of Representatives

CHIEF EXECUTIVES, 1829-(1987)

Governors and Administrators

1829	Lieutenant-Colonel Alexander Findlay	Lieut.	Governor
1830	George Rendall	"	"
1840	Sir Henry Huntley	"	"
1843	Captain H. F. Seagram, R.N.		Governor
1843	E. Norcott		"
1844	Commander G. Fitzgerald, R.N.		"
1847	Sir R. G. MacDonnell		"
1852	A. E. Kennedy		"
1852	Colonel L. S. O'Connor		"
1859	Colonel G. A. K. D'Arcy		"
1866	Admiral C. G. E. Patey, C.M.G.		Administrator
1871	T. F. Callaghan, C.M.G.		"
1873	Sir C. H. Kortright, C.M.G.		"
1875	Sir Samuel Rowe, K.C.M.G.		"
1877	Dr. V. S. Gouldsbury, C.M.G.		"
1884	Sir C. A. Moloney, K.C.M.G.		"
1886	Sir J. S. Hay, K.C.M.G.		"
1888	Sir Gilbert T. Carter, K.C.M.G.		"
1891	Sir R. B. Llewellyn, K.C.M.G.		"
1901	Sir G. C. Denton, K.C.M.G.		Governor
1911	Lieutenant-Colonel Sir H. L. Galway, K.C.M.G., D.S.O.		"
1914	Sir Edward J. Cameron, K.C.M.G.		"
1920	Captain Sir C. H. Armitage, K.B.E., C.M.G., D.S.O.		"
1927	Sir John Middleton, K.B.E., C.M.G.		"
1928	Sir Edward Denham, K.C.M.G., K.B.E.		"
1930	Sir H. Richmond Palmer, K.C.M.G., C.B.E.		"
1933	Sir Arthur Richards, K.C.M.G.		"
1936	Sir Wilfred T. Southorn, K.C.M.G., K.B.E.		"
1942	Sir Hilary Blood, K.C.M.G.		"
1947	Sir Andrew B. Wright, K.C.M.G.		"

1949 Sir P. Wyn Harris, K.C.M.G., M.B.E. Governor
1957 Sir Edward Windley, K.C.M.G., C.B.E. "
1962 Sir John Paul, M.C. "
1966 Alhaji Farimang Singhateh "

Gambian Chief Executives

1961 Pierre S. N'Jie, United Party Chief Minister
1962 Sir Dauda Jawara, People's Prog. Party Prime Minister
1970 "   "   "   "   "   " President

INTRODUCTION

The tiny Republic of the Gambia is situated in the extreme
western portion of the African continent surrounded on three
sides by Senegal. The boundaries of the Gambia are completely artificial, having nothing to do with natural ethnic or
geographic lines of demarcation. They were first drawn in
1889 during a meeting of French and British delegates in Paris
and were only slightly modified by later survey parties. The
boundaries thus agreed upon satisfied both European governments and were meant to be only temporary since both parties
were convinced that eventually there would be an exchange of
the Gambia. For a variety of reasons, no transfer ever took
place, and thus the half million Gambians are constrained
to live today in a country whose limits are roughly ten kilometers distant from either side of the Gambia River. These
lines exclude the Gambia from free access to its natural hinterland and divide the Gambian Wolof, Jola, Mandingo, and
Fulbe people from their kinsmen in Senegal.

The present day boundaries of the Gambia present specific problems for the historian. Much of the history of the
Gambia was not confined to the narrow serpentine state, but
extended over the broad savannah and sahel areas that today
comprise Senegal. This is particularly true of the period extending from the thirteenth through sixteenth centuries when
the Gambia Valley was being populated by a series of complex
migrations. Although little is known of the specifics, the
Wolof, Mandingo, and Fulbe people established themselves in
different sections of the Senegambia and there created first
village- or clan-based polities and finally large kingdoms.
These state building processes were still going on when the
first European traders came to the Senegambian coast. By the
opening of the seventeenth century, however, large complex
states had been created throughout the region with kings,
advisors, bureaucracies, and armed forces. The economic

1

basis of each of these states was village oriented agriculture,
although trade was important, particularly for those persons
who lived near the rivers or close by a hinterland trade route.

European contact with the Gambia region dates to 1455
when the Portuguese first entered the estuary of the river.
For over a century they maintained intermittent contacts with
the area, unchallenged by any European rival. During this
period a number of Portuguese chose to settle in the Gambia
and the government and the church sponsored missionary activities among the Mandingo. However, the Gambia was never
an important trading entrepôt and the Portuguese had decided
to concentrate their efforts elsewhere along the west coast
even before their trading monopoly was brought under attack
by other European states. During the early seventeenth century, few Portuguese traders came to the Gambia on a regular
basis. By the eighteenth century, the Portuguese interlude
was only dimly remembered by the people of the Gambia, and
the Portuguese left behind nothing of permanence.

The latter sixteenth century witnessed the continental
rivalries of European states which were invariably transformed
into worldwide conflicts. During the next two centuries, England, France, and Holland vied with one another for dominance
in the world's mercantile trade. Transferred to the Senegambia region, these European quarrels disturbed the general
peace, lowered profits and ultimately prevented any one state
from gaining a monopoly of the area's trade. At this juncture
it is important to note that the Senegambia was not an area
possessing great amounts of ivory, timber, pepper, or gold,
and thus was by-passed by the major thrust of European
trade in favor of more lucrative areas such as the Gold Coast.
Nevertheless, there were trading companies active in the Gambia from 1598 onward. As the slave trade became more important, European investment in ships, fixed goods, and trading
materials also increased in the Gambia.

The pattern for trade for all European states was dictated by mercantilism. Companies would be formed by stock-
holders who would receive a charter from a European monarch
giving them sole privileges to trade in a specific area. These
companies would then attempt to exploit their grant by sending
out to West Africa a wide variety of trade products to exchange
for African goods. In some areas the company men would be
forced to trade directly from their ships; in others they would

be allowed by the African rulers to build temporary trading stations, and in a few instances, such as along the Gold Coast, the Europeans manned a series of permanent fortified trading posts.

Although British trade in the Senegambia dates to 1553 and the French to 1560, the first permanent station in the Gambia was erected by citizens of the tiny Baltic principality of Courland in 1651. They purchased an island in the Gambia River which they named St. Andrew's Island and there constructed a fort. After a very brief interlude, the Courlanders were driven out by the English in 1661 who renamed the tiny island after James, Duke of York. James Island continued to be the center of English trading activities in the Gambia for over a century, first by the Royal Adventurers Trading in Africa, then the Royal African Company, and lastly by independent merchants.

French companies meanwhile had carved out a trading sphere further to the north, at the mouth of the Senegal River, and also opposite Cape Verde. St. Louis was founded in 1638, the island of Goree was taken from the Dutch in 1677, and the French established a station at Albreda opposite James Island in 1681. The eighteenth-century history of the French in the Senegambia is one of continual conflict with British elements on the Gambia River. For a brief period after 1760, the British controlled all French territory and created the Province of the Senegambia, only to return it all to France after the Treaty of Versailles in 1783. During the last stages of the American Revolution, a French combined force so completely destroyed the fort on James Island that it was never occupied again. British presence on the Gambia River in the last two decades of the eighteenth century was maintained by private traders without any definite official support for their activities.

All was changed by the British decision to abolish the slave trade as of January 1, 1808. It then became necessary to attempt to control the activities of British nationals along the western coast of Africa. For this purpose a part of the British navy was delegated to patrol the coastline. The force needed harbor facilities and this involved the British government directly in the administration of the Freetown Colony, and in 1816, Captain Alexander Grant was authorized to establish a base on the Gambia River. He rejected the old site

of British authority, James Island, and instead negotiated
the cession, by the king of Kombo, of St. Mary's Island,
adjacent to the south bank near the mouth of the river. In
the next four years, Grant and his small garrison of a few
hundred troops constructed administration buildings, harbor
facilities, and barracks on the island. Within months of its
beginning, the new town of Bathurst (today Banjul) had at-
tracted a considerable settlement of neighboring Africans.
In the 1820s and 1830s, the population of the area was greatly augmented by Wolof merchants from the Cape Verde area
and by Africans liberated from captured slave ships. In 1821,
the administration of the new Colony was taken from the Company of Merchants and vested in the Governor of Freetown.
Affairs in the Gambia were handled directly by an Administrator subordinate to the Governor. The size of the Colony
was increased in 1823 by the acquisition of MacCarthy Island
and in 1826 with the cession, by the ruler of Barra, of the
so-called Ceded Mile.

     European trade rivalry and the change in the fortunes
of one state or another had little to do with the lives of the
majority of Africans in the Senegambia. They, of course,
were affected by the volume, type, and direction of trade,
but direct relations with Europeans was not typical in the
Gambia. Economic changes in all the kingdoms were not revolutionary since the area never was a center for the slave
trade and there were few other products which the Europeans wanted. Thus the Mandingo polities along the river
and the Serer and Wolof states to the north continued to
evolve slowly with little outside interference.

     In the early nineteenth century, there were nine Man-
dingo kingdoms on the south side of the Gambia River:
Kombo, Foni, Kiang, Jarra, Niamina, Eropina, Jimara, Tomani, and Kantora. Along the north bank there were five
kingdoms: Niumi, Baddibu, Upper and Lower Niami, and
Wuli. Although each state was separate, and customs and
politics differed to a certain extent in each, all of them
shared certain commonalities. Each society was divided into
three endogamous castes: the freeborn, the artisans and
praise singers, and the slaves. Each state had a king
(mansa) chosen from a specific royal lineage. Each king
had his council of advisors and an armed force to defend
the state and with which, if necessary, he could impose his
will upon the state. Each kingdom was subdivided into

territorial units of the village, ward, and family compound.
Each village area was governed by a satiyo-tiyo, a representative of the senior lineage of the village, and his council. The ward leaders, or kabilo-tiyos, administered their
areas with the help of advisors. Thus each state was held
together by a combination of tradition, kinship patterns, and
force. The population of many of these kingdoms was relatively homogeneous, but some of the kings ruled over large
non-Mandingo minorities. There were Wolof and Serer in
Niumi and Baddibu, the Jola were located in Kombo and Foni,
and there were many Serahuli in the upriver kingdom of
Wuli. Large numbers of Fulbe had traditionally migrated
from the Futa Toro to the Futa Jallon through some of the
Mandingo states. By the mid-nineteenth century the Fulbe
had become a significant factor in the affairs of Eropina,
Jimara, Tomani, and Kantora.

To the north of the Gambia River were the larger,
more powerful polities of the Serer and Wolof. Each of the
Wolof states had evolved from the earlier kingdom of Jolof.
The Serer kingdoms of Sine and Saloum had evolved in the
same period with a mixed population. The Wolof and Serer
states, as the Mandingo, were of the Sudanic type with a
king representing a particular lineage, nobles who controlled
much of the land and who made up the king's councils and
commanded the armies, and peasants, artisans, and slaves.
Each polity maintained a large army and there was incessant
diplomatic maneuvering and open warfare between the states
because each king was jealous of his prerogatives and wanted
to dominate his neighbors.

In the nineteenth century all of the Senegambian kingdoms were subjected to new pressures and the intensification
of old cleavages. After mid-century, the French became
much more active in the hinterlands of the Senegambia. The
forward policy of Governor Faidherbe converted much of the
coastal region of Senegal into a practical French protectorate.
Peanuts had become an important item of trade, particularly
in Sine and Saloum, and French traders there demanded protection. Attempts to provide this embroiled the French in
the internal affairs of all the kingdoms north of the Gambia.
The British government, although disavowing territorial ambitions, nevertheless interfered continually in the affairs of
the Gambian kingdoms. From their base at Bathurst they
mounted a number of punitive expeditions against both the
traditional rulers and their Marabout challengers.

The most fundamental changes in the nineteenth century were introduced by proselytizing Muslim teachers. Islam had made slow but steady progress among the peoples of
the Senegambia during the previous two centuries. The religious revival which had wrought such great reforms in the
societies of Futa Toro, Macina, Futa Jallon, and northern
Nigeria reached the Senegambia by the 1850s. Seeking basic
religious, social, and political reforms, the Marabouts and
the growing number of their followers attacked the traditional Mandingo systems of rule in the kingdoms of the Gambia.
Thus began the half-century of internecine conflicts known
as the Soninke-Marabout Wars.

The first major test between the old order and the new
religious beliefs occurred in the south bank kingdoms of Kombo and Foni. In Kombo, Fodi Kabba of Gunjur, operating
with the followers of Omar of Sabaji from 1853 to 1855, conquered a large portion of the western section of the kingdom.
When the British Administrator, Colonel O'Connor, appeared
to favor the Soninke rulers, the Marabouts began planning
for the total negation of British power. In June 1855, the
Marabouts attacked the advanced elements of the British garrison and O'Connor and the bulk of his troops fell into a
trap laid by the Marabouts. After sustaining casualties of
over one-quarter of his force, the Administrator retreated to
Bathurst. Only with extreme difficulty and considerable reinforcements was he able to defeat the Marabouts. Although
O'Connor's final victory stabilized the British position, it ultimately did little to protect the traditional rulers, as yet
more people pledged their loyalties to Fodi Kabba, Fodi Silla,
and their lieutenants. The British would give no physical
support to the traditional rulers, contenting themselves with
intervening from time to time to arrange a truce between the
antagonists. The last of these interludes in open warfare
lasted for seven years after the truce of 1864. The final
test of strength of the two factions in Kombo occurred between 1871-75. In the latter year, the king, Tomani Bojang,
surrendered his last fortified town, accepted the peace terms
of Fodi Silla, and became a Muslim.

During the decade of the 1860s, Fodi Kabba shifted
the area of his activities to Foni and Kiang. Except in Jola
country, he and the other Marabouts were generally successful in imposing their will upon the poeple. The Jola, however, remained stubbornly independent and "pagan." Fodi

Kabba's forces did not receive a serious check in the other portions of these south bank kingdoms until they encountered the westward moving elements of the Fulbe armies loyal to Alfa and Musa Molloh. Eastern Kiang and western Jarra became for the rest of the century the rough dividing line between the territories controlled by Fodi Kabba and those by his enemies, the Mollohs.

The reforms demanded by the early Marabouts related specifically to the spread of Islam. They wanted to eradicate "pagan" influences and substitute for them a well ordered Muslim society. However, even at the beginning the movement drew to it a wide spectrum of protestors, many of whom were little concerned with the advancement of Islam. Throughout the Gambia the initial Marabout successes were tied to the military or political skill of a few men. As these men supplanted their Soninke enemies, they tended to lose their religious fervor and much of the warfare after 1870 was motivated primarily by personal or economic considerations with religion having little causative effect. Although this shift of emphasis is quite noticeable in the careers of Fodi Kabba and Fodi Silla, the best illustration of the secular nature of revolt against traditional authority is the career of the Mollohs in their state of Fuladu.

During the first half of the nineteenth century, there was an increasing influx of Fulbe into the south bank kingdoms of Tomani, Jimara, and Eropina. A Fulbe elephant hunter of Jimara who later took the name Alfa Molloh and was renowned for his ability with arms, quarrelled with his Mandingo overlord in the late 1860s. This began a revolt which, within five years, swept away the old system of government. In this phase as well as in later wars, Alfa Molloh counted heavily on the support of his fellow Fulbe rulers in the theocracies of Futa Toro and the Futa Jallon. It was believed that he had taken the Tijaniyya oath and had been created a deputy of Al Hajj Umar. Such rumors did not damage his image and were important in gaining Muslim adherents. However, the mantle of religious reformer rested lightly upon Alfa, and his son, Musa, was even less committed to the spread of Islam. They ranged themselves against Fodi Kabba, and in the 1880s, Musa consistently allied his state against the expansion of Ma Bâ's successors. Both the Mollohs were more concerned with the preservation of Fuladu, which they had created, than with advancing the cause of their religion against traditional "pagan" beliefs.

After Alfa's death in 1881, Fuladu was divided into two segments since by the Fulbe law of succession, the kingship was inherited by Musa's uncle, Bakari Dembel. Musa, who had led his father's armies, refused to accept completely this deposition and led his followers southward and established a fortified base in Hamdallai. He continued to pay nominal allegiance to his uncle, but it was Musa who was the real power in Fuladu. Finally in 1892, he moved against Bakari and proclaimed himself king of Fuladu. Long before this, Musa had created the best organized state in the Gambia. The highly centralized bureaucracy of the state placed almost absolute civil power in his hands. His control of the military forces assured Musa that his authority over his section of Fuladu was complete. This Fulbe autocracy would be altered only by the actions of the French and British.

The only serious attempt during the Soninke-Marabout Wars to establish a true theocracy of the type successfully achieved by Al Hajj Umar and Usuman dan Fodio was that of Ma Bâ, the ruler of Baddibu. Ma Bâ, a religious teacher, puritan, and Tijaniyya reformer, seized power in Baddibu in 1861, driving out the traditional rulers. Very soon he had gathered around him a significant number of believers, and with this force, attempted first to expand his control over Niumi. Here he encountered active opposition from the British and personally abandoned the forceful incorporation of that state into his kingdom. However, his lieutenant, Amer Faal, continued the Marabout conquests there, and by the 1880s, the bulk of Niumi was controlled by the Muslims.

Ma Bâ differed from most of his contemporary rulers because he envisioned himself always as the religious teacher and leader who was merely working out God's will in destroying the pagan kingdoms of the Senegambia. His armies were led by subordinates. Only once did his forces seriously attempt to gain a foothold on the south bank. In 1863, Ma Bâ authorized a large segment of his army to cross the river and attack the Soninkes in Kiang. In one of the major battles of the Soninke-Marabout Wars, Ma Bâ's forces were decisively beaten at Quinella. After this, Ma Bâ turned his full attention toward the overthrow of the Serer and Wolof states to the north.

In his attempt to create a large Senegambian theocracy, Ma Bâ was aided by the ex-rulers of Cayor, Macadou and Lat

Dior, and their followers. By early 1865, the bulk of Saloum
was under his control and that summer his forces conquered
Jolof. At this juncture his schemes were foiled by the
French. They had at first welcomed Ma Bâ since it appeared
that he was weakening the power of the traditional rulers in
Senegal. However, he had succeeded too well. The French,
who considered the entire Senegal as a trading sphere, did
not want a large powerful unified polity to take the place of
the divided, weaker traditional states. Governor Pinet-
Laprade of Senegal decided to halt Ma Bâ's advance and proceeded to Kaolack with approximately five thousand men. At
the battle of Pathebadiane in November 1865, the French and
their allies were narrowly defeated and forced to retreat.
Ma Bâ, however, was attempting too much with his limited
forces. He was supporting Lat Dior in southern Cayor and
Amer Faal in Niumi as well as maintaining forces in Saloum
and Jolof. In 1867, Ma Bâ decided to end the potential threat
of the Serer state of Sine and accompanied his army in its invasion. In the most crucial conflict of the Soninke-Marabout
Wars, the Sine forces defeated those of Ma Bâ and the pro-
phet teacher himself was killed.

The practical realization of the dream of a united Senegambia ended with Ma Bâ's death. Within a brief period,
Saloum and Jolof became independent and Baddibu itself was
rent by civil war. The chiefs of Baddibu selected Ma Bâ's
brother, Mamadou N'Dare, as the ruler, but within a decade
his rule was disputed by one of his lieutenants, Biram Cisse.
Soon afterward, Ma Bâ's son, Saër Maty, also claimed the
throne. In the armed conflicts which followed, Mamadou lost
most of his power and the kingdom was ruled by Biram Cisse
and Saër Maty. This state of affairs reduced Baddibu's
power to a mere cipher and made its absorption by the French
and British easy.

The continuing disturbances of the Soninke-Marabout
Wars interfered with trade and made the British possessions
on the Gambia River appear worthless to a Parliament and
Ministry devoted to saving money. All the administrators of
the Gambia were under orders to do nothing which would in-
volve the British in a major conflict in the hinterland. Thus
they acted against the Soninkes or Marabouts only when it
was impossible to avoid some kind of definite action and when
the chances of precipitating a larger conflict appeared minimal. Otherwise, the British were content to act as arbiters

in the conflicts. The Parliamentary Report of 1865 confirmed the no-expansion policy in the Gambia.

The French, however, since the governorship of Faid-herbe, had been purusing an aggressive trade policy in the independent Wolof and Serer states. The increasing value of the peanut crop aided the few, but ardent, French imperialists in Senegal and in France. These men saw a potentially great future for France in West Africa. Thus the governors of Senegal used what military forces they had to upset Wolof governments in Baol, Walo, and Cayor in order to blunt the westward ambitions of Al Hajj Umar and his son, Ahmadu, to build forts in Sine, Saloum, and Jolof, and to help defeat Ma Bâ's ambitions.

It is not surprising, therefore, that the French government should approach the British concerning an exchange of some French territory in return for the British possession on the Gambia River. The idea of such a trade was first suggested by the French in 1866. After four years of negotiations, almost all the details for an exchange had been completed when the onset of the Franco-Prussian War stopped all discussions. Internal difficulties in France postponed the resumption of negotiations until 1875. The French Foreign Ministry again found the British government receptive to their proposals. However, a combination of Parliamentary and commercial opposition from British and Gambian merchants halted the exchange. Despite this failure, the French government was convinced that, in time, Britain would cede the unwanted territory and France would be in possession of the Gambia River, the most economical highway to the interior of West Africa.

The "scramble" for Africa became a reality in the decade of the 1880s and the French began to occupy coastal areas which had long been considered British spheres. In Senegal they absorbed the coastal Wolof states and began in the late 1880s to interfere in the quarrels in Baddibu and Fuladu. The British government, spurred on by the urgings of the Gambian Administrators who believed that Britain was about the lose the Gambia by default, finally authorized the establishment of a Protectorate. In 1888, the Gambia was separated from the administrative control of Sierra Leone. In the following year, British and French representatives met in Paris to allocate spheres of influence in West Africa. The

British delegation was prepared to cede the Gambia provided the French would be more flexible in their demands elsewhere. When it became apparent that the French delegates were not prepared to compromise, the British demanded control of the river. British lack of interest in territorial acquisition in the Senegambia can be seen by their refusal to demand more territory than that represented by the narrow riverine strip which the French were willing to admit was a British sphere. However, neither power considered that the boundaries drawn by the Anglo-French Convention of 1889 were to be permanent.

Administrator Llewellyn had seen British policy change in the space of a few months from non-expansionist to expansionist. After the 1889 Convention he was charged with developing some suitable method of bringing law and order to the new Protectorate and devising a permanent system of government for the area. At first he could do little but announce the Protectorate and enter into generalized agreements with various Gambian chiefs. His first use of the military was in 1891 to protect the Anglo-French Boundary Commissioners from possible attack by Fodi Kabba and Fodi Silla. Later in January 1893, he assigned two Travelling Commissioners, one for the north bank and another for the south, to convey his orders and requests to the Gambian rulers. In the following year the government issued the first comprehensive Protectorate Ordinance. Although the full implications of this ordinance were not felt for some time, it established the form of government for the bulk of the Gambia which was to continue until just prior to independence. Later called "indirect rule," this system had the advantage of disturbing the Protectorate Gambians the least, and yet the British authorities at Bathurst could control overall political activities in the Protectorate by ordinances which were then enforced by their Commissioners.

The British and French Convention of 1889 in the Senegambia presented many of the Gambian rulers with almost insoluble problems. The accord meant for some the division of their kingdoms, forcing them to make a choice of which European government to accept as their overlord. To others, the establishment of European authority meant the abandonment of a life style which had been established for over a generation. Fodi Silla was the first to feel the changed nature of European activity. After he had been overawed by British gunboats in 1891, he remained quiescent until 1893, recognized by the British as the ruler of western Kombo. Then problems related to trade, particularly his participation in the slave trade, decided the British to invade his territory. In February 1894, his main base of Gunjar was taken and he was forced to flee to the Casamance. There he was arrested by French authorities and deported to St. Louis.

Fodi Kabba in 1892 retired to the' Casamance where he continued to support those Gambians dissatisfied with British rule. Periodically his followers would go on raids into the Gambia and retreat to French territory before effective pursuit could be organized. In 1900, at Sankandi, Travelling Commissioner Sitwell and other members of his party were killed. The town was known to be allied to Fodi Kabba, and the British and French subsequently decided to end his power permanently. A joint military venture was mounted in 1901, and in March of that year Fodi Kabba was killed.

Musa Molloh of Fuladu has decided in the early 1890s to live in peace with his neighbors and the Europeans. He chose to continue to live at Hamdallai in the Casamance and cooperated with the French. In 1901, he took part in the expedition against his old enemy, Fodi Kabba. However, his freedom from direct control has passed, and when the French decided to build a military post at Hamdallai, he burned the town and retreated with many of his followers to British Fuladu. There he was recognized as chief, received a stipend, and was generally left alone until after World War I. Then, reacting to rumors of his cruel and arbitrary actions, the British deposed him and sent him into exile. Four years later, in 1923, he was allowed to return, but was almost completely stripped of power in the small territory which the British allotted to him.

British assumption of power in the Gambia was largely without incident. Most Gambians were obviously exhausted by the half-century of wars and many welcomed peace. The system of "indirect rule" as developed in the twentieth century left almost unchanged the political and social systems which had existed prior to 1889. During the first 35 years of the twentieth century, there were enacted a series of Protectorate Ordinances which fixed the responsibilities of the state supported chiefs, the District Officers, and the central administration. In very general terms, the central govern-

ment, which was also that of the Colony area, comprised the
Governor, the appointive Legislative and Executive Councils,
the Secretariat, and the various departments such as Agriculture, Marine, and Public Works.   The central government
made all laws and regulations for the Protectorate and the
departments were responsible for work undertaken in the
areas of their jurisdiction in the Protectorate.   Government
in the Protectorate was carried on by a minimal number of
District Officers who supervised the work of the 35 recognized chiefs and who saw that the laws passed by the central government were carried out.

The key to social and economic development of the British system of rule in all Africa was the amount of money the
Treasury would appropriate.   The British Colonial Office followed a general rule that all territories had to live within
their budgets.   This meant that more economically viable territories such as Nigeria could expect considerable development of roads, transport, agriculture, and even education.
A small, poor area such as the Gambia was hard pressed just
to meet its recurrent budget.   Another facet of British financial administration was its conservatism.   Although the Gambia had acquired considerable cash reserves by 1918, these
funds normally were not used for development.   Thus few
improvements were made in the Protectorate until after World
War II when Colonial Development and Welfare funds became
available for the first time.   The Colony areas were more
fortunate.   In Bathurst, the port facilities were improved,
some streets were paved, there was a hospital, and the missionary groups maintained elementary and secondary schools
there.

The Gambia in the first half of the twentieth century
had progressed very little.   It was sustained by a single
export crop, peanuts, whose taxable value was just enough
to keep the government functioning.   Beginning in 1942, the
British government held out for the Gambia promises of a
better future when Colonial Development and Welfare funds
would become available.   These promises were never fully
realized, although some of the funds appropriated allowed
for improvements in the water supply, streets, and harbor
facilities of the capital city.   By 1947, it was apparent that
the moneys promised for improving Bathurst, building a new
government center, and modernizing the airport would not
be forthcoming.   The British government decision not to

improve Yundum airport meant that the worldwide air transport system would not have a major base in the Gambia. The
major airlines instead chose Dakar where the French were
more willing to invest in the necessary facilities. The Colonial Development Corporation wasted over Ł2 million between 1947-1951 in two schemes--the Yundum Egg Project
and the Rice Farm at Wallikunda. Each of these failed more
because of administrative error than any other factor. Nevertheless, the failures inhibited any further major development projects by the British for the Gambia. Thus in the
1950s, the Gambia was still dependent upon one crop, and its
communications and transport infrastructure were still primi-
tive. In the Protectorate there were no all-weather roads,
only one secondary school, and one hospital for over a
quarter of a million people.

     The post-World War II years elsewhere in British Africa
witnessed the rise of nationalistic movements which sought
greater African participation in government. This national-
ism, combined with the desire of the British government to
be rid of non-profitable areas, wrought a revolution in Africa
within a decade. The British began by making concessions
to the Western educated, middle-class Africans, recognized
African political parties, and eventually negotiated for the
independence of their African territories. In 1957, Ghana
became independent, in 1960 Nigeria, and in 1961 Sierra
Leone, leaving the Gambia as the only area in West Africa
still under British control. In the 1950s, there had been
some concessions which allowed more Gambian participation
in the central government. In 1947, 1952, and 1954, there
were changes in the size and composition of the Legislative
and Executive Councils. According to the provisions of the
1954 Constitution, Gambians held 16 of the 21 positions on
the Legislative Council and there was a form of Ministerial
government. Nevertheless, the real power resided in the
Governor and the higher administrative officers, almost all
of whom were English expatriates. The Protectorate government was still dominated by the District Officers and
the chiefs who were generally responsive to the wishes of
the Governor. All Protectorate representatives to the Legislative Council were chosen by indirect election.

     Political parties were formed very late in the Gambia
and they tended to reflect Colony interests and were normally the vehicles by which one man could be elected to the

Legislative Council. John C. Faye was instrumental in creating the Democratic Alliance in 1951, I. M. Garba-Jahumpa
formed the Muslim Congress later that same year, and in
1952 the supporters of P. S. N'Jie began the United Party.
These parties debated local Colony issues, and were prevented by law from campaigning in the Protectorate.

One of the major reasons for the lack of a national
policy was the confusion in almost every quarter about the
Gambia's future. It appeared that the territory was too
small and poor to consider independence as a viable goal.
Before the time of the independence of other British West
African territories, there was some consideration given to a
federal arrangement with another area. The Malta Plan was
also briefly considered as an alternative to direct control.
This envisioned a type of continuing political association between small, economically insecure parts of the Empire and
the British Parliament. After Malta opted for independence,
any hope that this scheme would work was given up.

The devolution of power to Africans in British territories represented a reversal of a philosophy of government
which had been dominant throughout the century. If any of
the new African states were to have a chance of economic
and political stability without serious alterations of its boundaries and general system of government, they had to be
ruled by Western educated men. Very few traditional rulers
had any type of Western education. Furthermore, indirect
rule was fundamentally divisive. Therefore, it could not be
used as a means of achieving national unity. It is ironic
that in the decade of the 1950s, the British government
turned over their rule to a group they had previously suspected and even disliked--the educated minority. In the
Gambia this process was particularly difficult for the Colonial Office since they had always supported the chiefs in
governing the Protectorate. Educated, Colony-based Gambians had been specifically prohibited from any type of political activity in the Protectorate. However, with the grant
of independence to other West African territories, the British could not refuse the demands of Gambian political parties
that the elective principle be extended to the Protectorate.
The Constitution of 1960 provided for direct elections for the
seven Colony and 12 Protectorate seats in the House. The
chiefs' powers to influence central policy were minimized since
they had the right to select only eight members of the Legislature.

A new political party, the Protectorate People's Party,
was formed in 1959 by a Protectorate veterinary officer,
David Jawara, and his associates. This party appealed most
directly to the Protectorate since its leaders were primarily
Mandingo and they stressed how much the Protectorate had
been ignored in the past. The United Party, led by P. S.
N'Jie, also expected to do well in the elections of 1960.
N'Jie had gained a considerable reputation in the 1950s as
an opponent of the policies of the British dominated government. The leaders of the other major parties, I. M. Garba-
Jahumpa and John C. Faye, joined their two parties together
just before the election to form the Democratic Congress Alliance. All parties campaigned vigorously throughout the
Protectorate, and despite the newness of the elective principle, there was very heavy voter participation in the elections of 1960.

Due to the nature of the Constitution, the elections
produced a veritable stalemate. Jawara's party, now renamed the People's Progressive Party, won eight Protectorate seats, the United Party gained five Colony and one Protectorate seat, and the Democratic Congress Alliance won
only three seats. The eight chiefs selected in an indirect
fashion thus became very important, not only for the composition of the House and in selecting the Ministers, but for
the appointment of a Chief Minister. Late in 1960, the Governor had indicated that he would appoint such an official.
Since the chiefs would not support Jawara and the PPP
refused to sanction a chief to hold this position, the Governor appointed P. S. N'Jie of the United Party as the Gambia's first Chief Minister. Jawara and the other PPP
ministers immediately resigned from the government.

It was very soon apparent that the 1960 Constitution
was not satisfactory to any of the Gambian factions. Two
Constitutional Conferences were held in May and July 1961,
resulting in a new instrument which provided for responsible government. The British in the new Constitution finally
abandoned support of the Protectorate chiefs. Thus in the
36-man House, the chiefs had only four indirectly elected
representatives while 25 members were to be directly elected
from the Protectorate. New elections were held in 1962, and
the results were a vindication of the claim of the People's
Progressive Party that the previous government was not
representative. They gained over 64 percent of all votes

cast and won 18 seats, while the United Party could gain
but 13. David Jawara became the Prime Minister, and the
People's Progressive Party exclusively formed the executive.
Even before the election of 1962, it was apparent that within
a short period the Gambia would receive its independence,
although there still existed serious doubts in Britain about
the ability of the area to afford that status. In 1963, the
Gambia received the grant of full self-government, and discussions were soon begun on the mechanisms of independence
and the date for this goal. Despite protests from the United
Party, the British government agreed with Jawara that there
was no need for new elections before the grant of independence. On February 18, 1965, the Gambia became an independent nation within the Commonwealth. Only four years had
elapsed since the Governor had agonized over the decision to
appoint a Chief Minister with very circumscribed powers.

Despite natural disasters, inflation, increasing costs
for imports, and a devastating coup attempt, Gambia since
independence has been an unexpected success story. The
People's Progressive Party government very early decided to
live within the limited financial resources of the country. It
maintains diplomatic relations with only Senegal, Britain, and
the United Nations. The salaries of ministers and members
of the House of Representatives are among the lowest in Africa. The development programs, although providing for the
all-weather trans-Gambian road, improved river transport,
and considerable progress in rice cultivation, have been
modest. The moderate economic policies of the government
of Sir Dauda Jawara (he changed his name and was knighted
in 1966), combined with an improvement in the price of peanuts enabled it to dispense with British grants-in-aid for
the recurrent budget during the 1970s. The drought years
of the late 1970s and early 1980s struck at this hard-won
economic independence and stability causing a balance of
payments problem and forcing the government to borrow from
outside sources. However, even here the frugality practiced
by the state has meant a minimization of economic dislocations.

The Gambia is one of the few states in Africa which
has remained faithful to the basic concepts of democratic
government. Although the potential of opposition parties has
declined drastically since independence this was more the
fault of the leadership of those parties than overt actions
taken by the ruling party. There has been no move by

President Jawara and his associates to restrict criticism or to create a one-party state. All attempts to form new political parties which could be viable alternatives to the PPP have failed to convince the electorate of a need for change. Sheriff Sisay, once Gambian Finance Minister, attempted in the late 1960s to challenge PPP dominance by forming the Progressive People's Alliance (PPA). It collapsed before the 1972 elections. More lasting was the National Convention Party (NCP) formed by a number of young Gambians and led by another former associate of Jawara's, Sheriff Dibba. Although it took the place of the United Party as the chief opposition, the NCP has never threatened seriously the hold that the PPP had on the government. In the 1982 elections following in the wake of the murderous coup attempt, the NCP could glean only 23 percent of the vote and secured five seats in the House. A new party headed by two of the President's former associates, Hassan Camara and Howsoon Samega-Janneh, was created in early 1986 but does not appear to be a serious threat to the ruling party.

One reason for the lack of success of rival political parties is the relative absence of issues. Most differences between the parties are minor and concern personalities rather than controversies. Two exceptions have been the republic issue and the question of closer association with Senegal. Many observers had considered some form of political association inevitable. Senegal, surrounding the tiny enclave, was larger, more economically advanced, and was composed of the same national groupings as represented in the Gambia. P. S. N'Jie and President Senghor in 1961 created the first inter-Ministerial committee to consult on problems connected with rapprochement. A United Nations Committee reported on the economic advantages in terms that indicated that in time such a political association was a foregone conclusion. However, the problems of language, law, education, and differential Western administration and customs could not be ignored. Neither could the substantial fears of Gambians that their interests would be submerged in any political association. Although much discussion had taken place and some economic and cultural agreements had been formed, a permanent political association seemed further away in 1980 than in 1965. There had been border clashes with Senegalese police and the differential tariff system of the two states was a continuing source of friction. But perhaps the prime reason was the improved economic position of the Gambia in comparison to Senegal.

Very soon after independence, Premier Jawara became
convinced that the Westminster form of government placed
him, as the practical ruler of the state, at a disadvantage
in dealing with other African leaders. The People's Progressive Party began a campaign to convince Gambians that a
Presidential form would solve this problem and give the Gambia a stronger government. When a plebiscite on this question was submitted to the voters in November 1965, they rejected the proposal by approximately 800 votes, and the government bowed to their wishes. The question was not resubmitted to the voters until 1970, and this time it was approved.
The Gambia then became a Republic on April 24, 1970, and
Sir Dauda became its first President. The decade of self-
rule under a responsible government had convinced many
Gambians, who earlier had thought otherwise, that they
could govern themselves, and therefore no particular advantage could be gained by a merger with Senegal.

All this was changed by what most observers had believed impossible--an attempted coup d'etat led by Kukio
Samba Sanyang, a disaffected leader of a radical socialist
movement. In retrospect there were earlier developments
which pointed toward the attempt. The worsening economic
conditions made many in Banjul receptive to radical ideas.
The small Socialist Revolutionary Party, the National Liberation Party, and the Gambia branch of the Movement for Justice in Africa (MOJA) had openly advocated the possibility of
violence. The Libyan government had invested heavily in
the Senegambia and it was known that a number of young
Gambians had been recruited for training in Tripoli ostensibly for subversive activity in West Africa. In late October 1980, the Deputy Commander of the Gambian Field Force
was killed by one of his men. The government linked this
to Libyan subversive activity and broke off diplomatic relations. Fearing further disturbances and betraying a lack
of confidence in the Field Force, President Jawara invoked
the 1967 mutual defense treaty with Senegal which responded
by sending 150 men to defend key installations near Banjul.
MOJA and the Social Revolutionary Party were banned and
some of the radical leaders were convicted of possessing weapons. The threat of radical violent activity appeared to have
been contained by early 1981 and the Senegalese troops were
withdrawn.

All appeared calm with no hint of political turmoil when
President Jawara travelled to London to attend the wedding

of Prince Charles. However, early in the morning of July
30, some members of the Field Force at Bakau seized the
arsenal, killed the senior officer present as well as some
police, and then marched on Banjul. On the way they
opened the gates to the prison releasing convicted criminals along with political prisoners. These were to be in
the forefront of much of the looting and violence which
wracked the capital during the following few days. The
revolutionaries seized the radio station and broadcast the
news that a new Revolutionary Council of 12 had been
formed to replace the deposed Jawara regime. By the evening the rebels controlled the roads into Banjul, the ferry,
and most of the city. One exception was the central police
station, which held out against all attempts to capture it.
The lack of planning and inability of Sanyang, heretofore
an unsuccessful and disgruntled political candidate, to control the direction of the coup can be seen in the looting of
many of the stores in Banjul and the indiscriminate firing
at people and property.

President Jawara in London was informed at mid-
morning of July 30 of the coup attempt and immediately flew
to Dakar. Even before he arrived, the Vice-President in
Banjul on instructions was conferring with President Diouf
and members of the government of Senegal. Once again the
1967 defense treaty came into effect and within hours members of the Senegalese army were converging on Banjul. By
July 31, a company of paratroops had captured Yundum airport and other main force units moved cautiously on the capital from the south by way of Lamin to Abuko to Serrekunda
thence to Denton Bridge. The Senegalese forces used ar-
mored vehicles with machine guns and these helped to keep
the fighting in Banjul to a minimum. Most of the skirmish-
ing took place on the way to the capital. By the time that
Banjul was secured other Senegalese units had recaptured
the ferry system at Barra and at Fera Fenni. In all, President Diouf committed over 600 troops to the initial phase of
action and the Senegalese lost 33 men, 17 in a helicopter
shot down by ground fire.

By August 2, the uprising had been contained and
President Jawara broadcast to the nation from Dakar that
evening. He accused Sanyang and his followers of unscru-
pulous use of young and impressionable people and criminals
to carry out orders directed from elsewhere. The President

appealed to the rebels to lay down their arms with the assurance that they would be treated humanely. However, he
threatened terrible retribution in Bakau if any of the hostages who had been taken early in the fighting, presumed to
number over one hundred, should be harmed. This warning
had a poignant, personal meaning since one of the President's
wives and four of his children were being held by the rebels
in one of the Medical Research Council buildings at Bakau.
President Jawara returned to the Gambia on August 2, and
the hostages at Bakau, including members of the President's
family, were rescued two days later. Members of the cabinet
met on that same day signalling to the world that the rebellion was at an end.

    The capital was a shambles. A reporter for the Dakar
newspaper, Le Soleil, wrote, "There was desolation and
death, smoking ruins of buildings half burnt-down, wrecked
vehicles, rotting corpses, pavements piled with rubbish of
every kind." Stores had been looted, the old law court
buildings were all but destroyed, and the walls of most structures along Wellington Street were pockmarked with bullet
holes. Then there were the dead. The actual count will
probably never be known. Official estimates soon after the
pacification placed the number at near 600, observers at
Victoria Hospital estimated 800, and some officials later agreed
that the number might well reach one thousand. From later
reports it was obvious that many old scores, totally uncon-
nected with political issues, had been paid off during the
first few hours when the capital appeared open to anyone
with a gun.

    Some of the leaders of the rebellion were killed, a few
including the leader, Sanyang, escaped to Guinea-Bissau,
but most were captured by the Senegalese. Ultimately 1,024
persons were detained, accused of taking part in the insur-
rection. The most distinguished of the prisoners were two
members of the legislature, former Vice-President Sheriff
Dibba and Gibou Jagne of the NRC. The government proclaimed a state of emergency and established a curfew on
the citizens of Banjul. The curfew remained in force for 14
months and the emergency was not lifted until December 1982.
Most of the Senegalese troops had left the Gambia by the
time Parliament met in mid-August 1981, but a number remained behind to provide security for Government House,
the airport, the prison, and Denton Bridge. Their presence

was a constant reminder to the Gambians of the coup attempt
and the weakness of the Gambia.

The issue of a closer formal political association between Gambia and Senegal, which had been avoided for 15
years, could no longer be ignored. President Diouf of
Senegal was criticized heavily by some segments of the opposition for his actions in sending army units to the Gambia.
He needed to have some assurance from the Gambia that the
association issue would be clarified. In the weeks which followed, President Jawara could not afford to dispense with
the Senegalese troops. It was in this context that the discussions on closer association began. In August 1981 the
intent to create a confederation was announced and President Jawara toured the country to explain the proposed
union. In November a formal declaration was issued at Kaur
and by the following month, working parties from the two
states had agreed upon the details of the union. On December 29, both the Senegalese and Gambian legislatures approved the new treaty and the Confederation of the Senegambia was born. Later protocols setting up the Confederation were filed as required with the United Nations.

Coordination could be achieved much easier between
Gambian and Senegalese members of the Executive. The
President of Senegal became the President of the Confederation while the Vice President was the President of Gambia.
The areas to be addressed first by the Confederation planners were financial cooperation and foreign affairs. Each of
the Presidents already had considerable discretionary powers
in dealing with these subjects. Although even under the
best of circumstances it would take years to rationalize the
differing financial and economic policies of the two areas, it
would be easier to achieve agreement even in these complex
areas because they demand only the concurrence of the
President and Vice President of the Confederation. But even
here there are significant questions to answer before any-
thing more than the semblance of a confederation policy can
be achieved. It appears that many Senegalese politicians
consider it to be only a matter of a brief time span before
confederation gives way to a unitary government. Such
opinions openly expressed have added to the fears of many
Gambians. Although the confederation instruments were approved by a voice vote of all the PPP members of the House
on December 29, there was some doubt even then that all

were enthusiastic about any agreement which would ultimately relegate Gambia to a secondary position in a confederation
dominated by a French-speaking majority.

The agreements also called for a Confederation Parliament to be established which would be given authority to
legislate on matters common to the two areas. As envisioned,
this Parliament was to convene twice a year and could also
be called into special session if the situation warranted and
if requested by one-third of the members. This was in all
probability a concession to the Gambia which was guaranteed
one-third of the seats in the proposed Parliament. The half-
decade since the creation of the Confederation has seen little
movement toward the establishment of a functioning joint Parliament or for more than improved communications between
Presidents Jawara and Diouf. There have been signs of im-
patience on the part of Senegalese officials on the slowness
of implementing the agreement as well as a deepening of sus-
picion on the part of Gambians afraid that their state will be
submerged into the larger Francophone Senegal. In early
1986 Gambian officials reacted sharply to the action of the
Senegalese ambassador to the United Nations issuing visas
for the Gambia without prior consultation with the authorities in Banjul.

Reconstruction work on the wrecked capital was begun
immediately and within a year there were few physical evi-
dences of the murderous coup attempt. For most Gambians,
life soon resumed its normal pace. President Jawara's government, although it had maintained itself by the interposi-
tion of an outside force, began to function in basically the
same manner as before the attempted coup. The only major
change was in the degree of security provided for the President and working staff at Government House. As time
passed, the pressing problems of the economy and the onset
of drought conditions once again took precedence over the
political issues of the coup attempt and confederation. Many
Gambians in Banjul found the continued presence of the Senegalese increasingly offensive and all of the old reasons for
resisting a practical closer union with Senegal resurfaced.

However improbable the state of the Gambia might have
seemed to some in 1965, it has shown a political maturity un-
matched by most other African states. This has enabled the
Gambia to surmount the economic difficulties of its first two

decades of independence and its moderate government to survive a bloody coup attempt. Although prognostication concerning the future of any African polity is risky, it does appear that this area, demarcated almost as an afterthought by two European powers in 1889, has an excellent chance of survival.

THE DICTIONARY

AHMADIYYA.   A Pakistan-based sect of Islam created in the
19th century by Hazrat Mirza Ahmad.   Its major theme is
the reconciliation of Islam and Christianity.   In the last
four decades, active proselytizing by missionary teachers
has converted many Africans, particularly in coastal towns,
to this belief.

AKU.   A title given to the Yoruba recaptives.   It has been
misused by some observers to mean all the recaptives' Westernized descendants and non-Gambian African residents in
the Colony areas.   In the Gambia, the Aku in the late 19th
and 20th centuries came to exercise an influence far beyond
their numbers.   They adopted Western modes of living, accepted Christianity, and educated their children in Sierra
Leone and Great Britain.   The Aku became successful traders, entered the civil service, and in the period between
1945 and independence came to dominate many of the important government positions in the Gambia.

ALBREDA.   Today a small river-port village located in upper
Niumi.   It was for a long time the trading center for the
French in their efforts to dominate the Gambia River trade.
The French Senegal Company first obtained trading rights
to that portion of the north bank area in 1679, and Albreda was established two years later opposite the English
station on James Island.   During the century-long period
of wars between England and France, Albreda was looted
and abandoned many times.   The French retained their
proprietary rights to the area until the Convention of 1857
with Britain gave them exclusive rights to Portendic in return for relinquishing their claims to Albreda.

ALKALI.   A title given to an African ruler's representative
to a European trading area.   In time, it came to mean to
the Mandingo the same as satiyo-tiyo or a village head.

25

ALMAMY. The spiritual leader in Muslim societies who was
concerned with prayer, education, and general religious
rule making. In many Mandingo villages there was a type
of dual control between the religious leader and the alkali,
the secular leader.

AMER FAAL. One of the chief lieutenants of Ma Bâ in the
Kombo and Ceded Mile areas between 1864-66. The difficulties there were precipitated by the British decision to
allow refugees from the wars in Saloum to settle in the
Ceded Mile area. In 1866, Amer Faal's continual raids re-
opened the question of British supremacy along the lower
north bank territory. In 1866, a large mixed British expedition was mounted against Amer Faal and the Marabouts.
Albreda was taken without casualties, but Amer Faal's main
stockaded base, Tubab Kolon, was taken by storm.

ANGLO-FRENCH CONVENTION, 1882. The culmination of
over three years effort by the British Foreign Office which
wanted a clear demarcation of British and French spheres
of influence in West Africa. The Convention granted most
of the French claims along the coast between Conakry and
Freetown, and called for both Britain and France to maintain the status quo. Implicit in the Convention was the
desire to rectify spheres of influence, and this very clearly
meant an exchange of the Gambia for some suitable territory elsewhere. Although the British Foreign Office continued for some time to recognize the status quo, the Convention never became effective because the French Chamber
of Deputies refused to ratify the agreement.

ANGLO-FRENCH CONVENTION, 1889. The result of British
pressures begun in 1887 to have a specific understanding
with the French government on delimitation of territory in
Senegambia. By the close of 1888, the French were presented in a number of places along the banks of the Gambia River, and British authorities in the Gambia had begun
to collect treaties with riverine rulers. In April 1889, a
high level series of meetings began in Paris with the object
of warding off any possible conflict between the agents of
the two powers in the Gambia, Sierra Leone, Ghana, and
Nigeria. The Convention as signed did establish coastal
boundary lines between the spheres of influence of the
two powers in all of these areas, but the agreement had
more far-reaching ramifications for the Gambia than for

any of the other areas in western Africa. E. H. Egerton
of the Foreign Office and Augustus Hemming of the Colonial Office represented Britain while the French delegates
were M. Nisard, Director of Protectorates of the Foreign
Ministry, and M. Bayol, Governor of Senegal. The British
delegates at first tried to obtain a clear cut demarcation of
spheres of influence in western Africa. Failing in this,
they decided to force the French to recognize their claims
to both banks of the Gambia River and thus they conceded
the hinterland of the Gambia to French control. At the
third general session, this limited British objective was
gained when the French delegates admitted in principle
that the Gambia was a British river. M. Bayol drew two
lines upon a map from the mouth of the river to Yarbutenda and stated that within these lines was the territory
that could be reasonably assigned to Britain. Ultimately
the two parties agreed on British occupation rights to the
banks of the Gambia ten kilometers north and south of the
river as far inland as Yarbutenda and there the eastern
boundary of the Gambia was to end on a ten kilometer radius drawn from the center of the town. Both the French
and the British negotiators considered the agreements
reached regarding the boundaries of the Gambia to be only
temporary. The British believed that in the future they
would be able to trade their exclusive rights to the down
river areas for concessions by the French elsewhere in
Africa or in the world. The French believed that in time
the British government would realize the non-viable char-
acter of their new Protectorate and would be more than
willing to allow it to be absorbed by Senegal. Neither of
these prognoses proved to be correct. The decade following the Anglo-French Convention of 1904 saw both governments unwilling to test the new found entente by raising
embarrassing questions about an area which neither party
considered to be very important. Thus the boundary
agreed upon in 1889 and demarcated on the ground in the
1890s became the permanent boundary between the Gambia
and Senegal.

ANGLO-FRENCH CONVENTION, 1904. This most important
agreement cleared the way for the entente between France
and Britain which was to have such fateful consequences
for European peace in the summer of 1914. The agreement
finally settled the most outstanding differences between
the two states regarding fishing rights off Newfoundland,

spheres of influence in northern Africa, and border disputes in western and central Africa. Article five of the
agreement ceded Yarbutenda to France with the stipulation that if the Gambia River was not navigable for sea-
going vessels at that point, then the French would be
given access to territory lower down on the Gambia River.
Although the Convention was very explicit on this point,
the British Foreign Office later resisted the claims made
by the French for such mid-river enclaves. The excuse
of the British for delaying action on the French demands
for a river port was that such an enclave would allow the
French to draw off the bulk of the peanut exports and
thus Bathurst and the British Protectorate would be even
more poverty stricken than was then the case. Although
the French government in the period from 1906 to 1910
were very active in pressing for the mid-river port and
some of their officials in Senegal revived the plans for an
exchange of territories, they were very careful not to allow this question to endanger the new found but shaky
friendship between Britain and France. The thrust of
French policy in the early part of the 20th century was
to gain support for what they considered to be their inevitable confrontation with Germany in Europe. After
1910, the French government ceased to press Britain for
territorial enclaves on the Gambia or exchanges of territory. The first World War and the building of the railway and road system in Senegal, and the concentration
of French capital in the ports of Kaolack and Ziganchour
made the possession of the Gambia less important to
France. After 1918, virtually all diplomatic activity concerning an exchange of territory for the Gambia ceased.
Thus the boundaries established in 1889 which had been
considered temporary expedients became permanent political realities.

ANTONIO, PRIOR OF CRATO. In the period after 1580,
one of the claimants to the Portuguese throne. Phillip II
of Spain, the champion of Catholicism and the enemy of
England, had in that year amalgamated the thrones of
Spain and Portugal. The Prior, believing himself to be
the true king of Portugal, rented certain trading concessions in Portuguese territory to English merchants. It
was on the basis of these concessions that Queen Eliza-
beth in 1588 granted exclusive trading rights for a period
of ten years to certain English merchants trading in West

Africa. The company which was thus formed was the first
organized effort on the part of the English to exploit the
imagined wealth of western Africa.

ARCHER, FRANCIS BISSET. Government official and author,
posted to the Gambia from Nigeria in January 1903, as
Colonial Treasurer. He also served as acting Colonial
Secretary in 1904 and 1905, and briefly in 1905 was the
acting Governor of the Gambia. In 1905, he authored
the first book specifically devoted to the Gambia entitled,
The Gambia Colony and Protectorate: An Official Hand-
book.

ARMITAGE, SIR C. H. Governor of the Gambia from 1920
to 1927. He was in charge of administration during the
recession following World War I and was partially responsible for the slowness in recalling from circulation the
French five franc piece. This demonetization crisis ultimately cost the Gambia over £200,000. Governor Armitage's main positive contributions to the Gambia were the
establishment of the Agriculture Department in 1924 and
the founding of a secondary school for the sons of chiefs
at Georgetown in 1923.

ARMITAGE SCHOOL. Established by Governor Armitage at
Georgetown in 1923 as a school for the sons of chiefs.
Intended to give its students the rudiments of reading
and writing, it long catered to the Protectorate aristoc-
racy. In the 1920s there were only two main elementary
schools for the Protectorate. One was a Catholic school
at Basse, and the other a Wesleyan school at Georgetown.
There was, therefore, little demand for more secondary
school facilities until after World War II. The expansion
of all education in the postwar years dictated improvements to Armitage. It became a boarding post-primary
school, the only one in the Protectorate. In 1961 its
facilities were expanded to accommodate 200 pupils.

ASSOCIATION FOR THE DISCOVERY OF THE INTERIOR
REGIONS OF AFRICA. An organization created in 1788
by Sir Joseph Banks and other Englishmen with similar
curiosity about the unexplored parts of the world. Of
particular interest to the Association was the question of
the existence of the Niger River. If it existed, where
was its source, in what direction did it flow, was it

connected with the Gambia, Senegal, and Nile Rivers,
and what was its outlet? The Association first sponsored two expeditions, one to cross the Sahara from
North Africa, and the other from Egypt. Both ended in
failure. They next commissioned Major Houghton who set
out from the Gambia in November 1790, to penetrate the
mysteries of the western Sudan. He was killed after ac-
complishing little that he had expected to achieve. The
most successful venture sponsored by the Association was
that of the young Scottish physician Mungo Park, who in
December 1795 left the upper river station of Pisania on
the Gambia. Park eventually reached Segu on the Niger
before being forced to turn back. His two and one-half
year journey was the first successful European exploration of the interior of Africa and helped the Association
convince the British government to support further exploration.

-B-

BÂ, MA (also known as Amad Bâ or Maba). The son of
N'Dougou Pende Bâ, a Koranic teacher in a largely Wolof
area of Baddibu. Ma Bâ received Koranic education in
Cayor, and then later taught the Koran in Jolof. While
in Jolof, Ma Bâ married the niece of the Burba Jolof and
thus forged ties with the premier Wolof state. After his
father's death, Ma Bâ returned to Baddibu to assume his
father's responsibilities. Probably in 1850, Ma Bâ had his
only meeting with Al Hajj Umar at the village of Kabakoto,
and at the conclusion of that meeting, Ma Bâ was chosen
as the Tijaniyya representative in Baddibu.
    During the decade of the 1850s, Ma Bâ continued teach-
ing the Koran in Baddibu. There is some confusion as to
why he turned from such peaceful activities. The most
likely conclusion is that he, an Islamic teacher with considerable following among the people of Baddibu, was
caught up in a clash between the Mandingo rulers and the
British. In 1861, the British decided to punish the king
of Baddibu for his harassment of Bathurst traders. Governor D'Arcy coordinated his offensive against Baddibu
with the efforts of the French moving through Saloum, and
the king of Baddibu was quickly defeated. Presumably
Ma Bâ had aided the British in the course of their invasion and had helped to arrange the peace terms. After

the war, the king of Baddibu decided to rid himself of
this potential enemy with such a large Muslim following
and sent his son to kill Ma Bâ. Instead, the son was
killed by Ma Bâ's followers and the revolt in Baddibu began. Within a short period of time, the Marabout forces
had overcome their Mandingo overlords, the king was
killed, and large numbers of his followers forced into
exile.

The success of Ma Bâ's revolt caused other Marabouts
on the north bank to look to him for aid, and in May 1862,
Ma Bâ sent his army into Niumi to aid his fellow Muslims.
An invasion of Baddibu by the Bur Saloum forced Ma Bâ
to retreat. Later he recognized the independence of Niumi with the stipulation that it pay him a tribute through
his lieutenant, Amer Faal. In the subsequent campaigning against Saloum, Ma Bâ was generally successful so that
by the fall of 1863, the Marabout forces responsive to Ma
Bâ controlled most of the territory between the Gambia
and the Saloum rivers except a part of Niumi.

Ma Bâ's sphere of influence extended northward into
eastern Saloum as far as Jolof. Unlike many of the other
war chiefs or Marabouts of the Senegambia, Ma Bâ was
motivated primarily by the hope of creating a large, viable Islamic state. He was, like Usuman dan Fodio and
later Muhammad Ahmed, the director of a religio-political
movement rather than merely a warrior. Ma Bâ's desires,
however, ran counter to the plans of the French who were
concerned with dominating the trade of the Serer states of
Sine and Saloum. The anxiety of the French administrators and traders was increased by the conversion of Macadou and Lat Dior, both ex-damels of Cayor, who had
been replaced by the French because of their opposition
toward French policies. The French at first welcomed Ma
Bâ's activities since he was weakening the power of the
Wolof and Serer tyeddos. In October 1865, the French
by treaty recognized Ma Bâ as the Almami of Baddibu and
of Saloum, and he agreed to respect the rights of French
traders already in Saloum. In June 1865, Ma Bâ sent his
forces northward into Jolof and within a few months he
was in almost complete control of that Wolof state. A revolt in Saloum forced him to devote his total attention
again to the south and doomed his plans for a union with
the Trarza Moors to the north of the Senegal River. In
November 1865, the French governor, Pinet-Laprade, disturbed over Ma Bâ's power and influence, led a large

army reported to be upwards of 5000 men overland to strike at Ma Bâ's forces near Kaolack. The battle of Pathebadiane appears to have gone in favor of the Marabouts, and Pinet-Laprade withdrew his forces northward.

During 1866, Ma Bâ's position in Jolof and the area around Kaolack declined as he was supporting Lat Dior in the invasion of southern Cayor and also his lieutenant, Amer Faal, in action against Niumi. Despite his weakened position, however, Ma Bâ planned to rid himself of the kingdom of Sine, the last Soninke state standing between his kingdom and the French. After the rains began in 1867, Ma Bâ accompanied his army in an invasion of Sine. The Serer tyeddo in a major battle at Somb repulsed the invading forces. Lat Dior fled the area, and after the battle, Ma Bâ's body was discovered on his prayer mat. With Ma Bâ's death,the most critical threat to European power in the Senegambia ended. He had come very close to restoring the old Jolof empire by utilizing the militant forces of Islam which he discovered in Baddibu, Saloum, and Jolof. None of his successors or any other Gambian leader came close to unifying the Senegambia. Ironically, the wars launched by Ma Bâ had weakened the Senegambian states to the extent that the French and British found little resistance to their further penetration of the interior in the following two decades.

BÂ, MAMADOU N'DARE. Chosen by the chiefs of Baddibu to succeed his brother, Ma Bâ, in 1867. Before the wars on the north bank, he had studied the Koran in Mauritania and helped Ma Bâ run a school in Jolof. Like his brother, he was austere and a good puritanical Muslim. He continued the wars begun by Ma Bâ along the Gambia River and reached the apex of his power when he controlled loosely much of the north bank from the Atlantic to Wuli. The British signed a treaty with him, recognizing his hegemony in all those areas except Niumi. However, his Marabout forces were not able to conquer Sine and the inland Wolof territories where the French had become dominant. Mamadou was not successful in establishing permanent institutions of government which could keep his war chiefs in check and in 1877 one of them, Biram Cisse, decided to build his own fortified base and refused Mamadou's order to tear down the walls of his town. This began a devastating civil war which was to last until the French invasion of 1887, when those territories farthest

from Nioro were freed from Mamadou's control. Musa Molloh and the Bur Saloum allied themselves with Cisse and
by the early 1880s, Mamadou had lost most of the territory over which he had ruled. His problems were further
complicated by the actions of Saër Maty, Ma Bâ's son, who
claimed the kingship created by his father. In 1886, the
British withdrew the stipend paid to Mamadou as ruler of
Baddibu. Cisse and Maty had almost reached an agreement where Cisse recognized the younger man as suzerain
in that year, but each wanted the stipend which Governor
Carter decided to pay to neither. The conflict continued
into the next year when French forces defeated the Marabouts, forced Saër Maty to flee, and divided what was
left of Ma Bâ's patrimony between Cisse and the aged
Mamadou. Once again king, if only over a small area, by
the grace of the French, Mamadou lived to enjoy this
shadow power until his death in 1889.

BÂ, SAËR MATY. Son of Ma Bâ. His mother was the niece
of the Burba Jolof. Although a council of chiefs had selected his uncle, Mamadou N'Dare Bâ, to succeed Ma Bâ
as ruler of the kingdom of Rip, Saër Maty never gave
wholehearted support to the new ruler. He had gained
considerable influence by the early 1880s because of transferred allegiance from his father and also because of his
leadership qualities. It is probable that he was the real
power behind Mamadou before the latter was so badly defeated by Biram Cisse. In the mid-1880s, Saër Maty was
involved in a series of wars with Cisse over control of the
riverine areas of Baddibu. It appeared briefly in 1886
that Cisse would accept the overlordship of Saër Maty
and peace would come to the north bank. However, the
war continued, and in 1887, the French, fearful of an extension of the war to Saloum, decided to pacify the territory. In April 1887, the French, reinforced by the tyeddo
of Saloum, defeated Saër Maty's forces a number of times,
forcing him to flee to British protection in the Ceded Mile.
The British, concerned with French operations so near the
Gambia River, refused to surrender Saër Maty and he continued to live quietly in a village near Bathurst until his
death in 1897.

BADDIBU (or, Rip). Today a section of the Gambia located
on the north bank which stretches roughly from the town
of Salakini to just below the town of Ballangar in lower

Saloum. The bulk of the present day population of
Baddibu is Mandingo, although there is a significant
concentration of Wolof in upper Baddibu. In the 19th
century, Baddibu was one of the most important of the
Gambian kingdoms. In the 1860s, Ma Bâ used Baddibu
as his base in attempting to create a large Islamic kingdom. At its greatest extent, the kingdom of Baddibu,
or Rip, comprised not only the present day riverine
areas, but also Saloum, parts of Cayor, and Jolof.

BADGE MESSENGERS. Created by a Protectorate Ordinance
in 1909 which gave chiefs and certain headmen the right,
with appropriate permission from the British authorities,
to appoint men to keep the peace in a given area. They
were called Badge Messengers because of the peculiar
symbol of authority they were authorized to wear. They
had all the rights, duties, and liabilities of the regular
police who operated in the Colony area. Although conditions in the Protectorate changed drastically in the fifty
years after they were authorized, Badge Messengers remained the local constabulary which enforced the decisions
of the Native Authorities down to the very eve of independence.

BADOLO. Wolof term for a poor peasant. Normally it referred to someone who was not a slave nor did he belong
to a caste. Although free, he had no wealth or power
nor claim to a political title. He had the right to farm
his land and pass it on to his sons. He owed a share of
his harvest to the local chief (Laman) and military service and other minor duties. The word "Badolo," although
Wolof in origin, came to be applied by other ethnic groups
in the Senegambia to persons of similar status.

BALDE, ALFA MOLLOH EGUE. The creator of the state of
Fuladu and one of the main participants in the Soninke-
Marabout Wars in the upper river during the 1870s. A
member of the Fulbe Firdu, he was born Molloh Egue in
the old Mandingo kingdom of Jimara, probably in the
third decade of the 19th century. He was an elephant
hunter, and had gained a great reputation with arms before a disagreement with the ruler of Jimara caused him
to lead a revolt of the Fulbe against the traditional rulers.
It was rumored that he had met with Al Hajj Umar and
had taken the Tijaniyya oath before 1867. His devotion

to Islam, however, appears to have been more a matter of
expediency than true devotion. It did gain him support
from the Islamic states of the Futa Jallon and Futa Toro.
His forces in a five-year period conquered Jimara, Tomani,
and a number of smaller chieftaincies southward to the
Casamance, and then laid the foundations for the centralized state of Fuladu, constructed largely with the conquests of his son Musa. Molloh Egue, soon after his initial conquest, assumed the name of Alfa Molloh. Alfa did
not hesitate to use armed forces to subdue potential rivals,
and his chief agent in establishing control over the Fulbe
was Musa and his army. After Alfa's death in 1881, Fuladu was torn by internecine strife because according to
the matrilineal succession, Alfa's brother, Bakari Dembel,
inherited the throne.

BALDE, MUSA MOLLOH. The son of Alfa Molloh, founder of
the Fulbe kingdom of Fuladu. During the decade of the
1870s, Musa was content to act as the commander of his
father's military forces, and it was he more than any other
person who expanded the areas under the control of Alfa
at the expense of the traditional Mandingo rulers as well
as those of such other Marabouts as Fodi Kabba and Simotto Moro. The death of Alfa Molloh in 1881 fractured
the recently created state of Fuladu since Musa had no
intention of meekly surrendering his power to his uncle
who had inherited the throne. Musa took his faction
southward, established a fortified base at Hamdallai, and
in 1883 placed himself under the protection of the French.
With their aid he soon reestablished his authority throughout much of Fuladu, and eventually killed his uncle and
other members of the family who stood in his way of maintaining control of the state. Finally in 1892, he proclaimed
himself king. The state which Musa Molloh created was a
reflection of his need for a stable kingdom which would
respond quickly to his desires. He exercised complete
military authority and controlled the political life of the
state by a close watch over the 40 district leaders he appointed to act in his name throughout the territory. Musa
also used a central bureaucracy to check on the activities
of the district heads. Unfortunately for Musa's centralized state, the partition of the Senegambia after 1889
brought fundamental changes to Fuladu. It was clear to
Musa that in order to maintain the unity of his kingdom,
he would have to choose peace rather than war with the

Europeans, and he therefore promised to live quietly in
the newly established French territory. In 1901, he participated in the joint expedition against his old enemy,
Fodi Kabba. However, with the arrival of more French
and British authorities in the interior, the days of his
freedom of action were almost at an end. The French
interfered more and more with his rule, particularly as
the rumors of his tyranny against his subjects reached
the centers of authority. In 1903, the French decided
to build a military post at Hamdallai. In response, Musa
burned his town, cut the telegraph lines, and retreated
to British territory where he established himself at Kessellikunda. The British recognized his control over what
was then only a small portion of his once large kingdom.
They paid him an annual stipend and in general left his
rule alone. Without an army and cut off from the bulk of
his previous territory in the south, he was actually a
British prisoner. They could depose him whenever they
wished. It was merely to their advantage to have such a
strong ruler who acted as a unifying force in the upriver
areas. In 1919, finally reacting to reports of atrocities,
the British deposed Musa, pulled down his royal compound,
and exiled him to Sierra Leone. He was allowed to return
in 1923, shorn almost entirely of his power. Until his
death in 1931, he remained nothing but a shadowy reminder of the time when he was the most powerful of the kings
of the southern Senegambia.

BALDEH, PAUL LOUIS. Teacher and politician, born to a
Fulbe family at Sare N'Gai in 1937 and educated at local
Catholic mission schools and at the Catholic Secondary
School at Banjul. In 1954, he attended Dublin University
and received a B.A. degree and returned to teach at the
Banjul Catholic Secondary School. He early aligned himself with the People's Progressive Party and resigned his
teaching position to campaign for the party in the upriver
Fulbe areas. He was elected to the House of Assembly in
1962, and received the portfolio of Minister of Education.
Difficulties developed within the party and Baldeh was
dismissed in 1963. However, just before independence,
he was again appointed Minister of Education. He was reelected to the House in 1966, but was passed over for a
further ministerial post.

BANJUL. The name initially given to the island ceded by

the King of Kombo in 1816 to Captain Alexander Grant,
who immediately set his men building houses and barracks
at a site on the island where a fort could help control entrance into the Gambia estuary. Grant renamed the island
St. Mary's and the new town, Bathurst, in honor of the
then Secretary of State. Banjul Island thus became the
center of British activity in the Gambia and the most pop-
ulous portion of the Colony. In 1973, the government of
President Jawara decided to change the name of the capital city to one without the connotations of the Colonial
past. In mid-1985 the capital city had a population in
excess of 50,000 persons and remained the chief port and
site of government.

BANTABA. A meeting place, usually a raised platform under
a shade tree in each yard or village where the elders and
the village head would come together to discuss matters
of concern and to arrive at consensus decisions.

BANTO FARO. A Mandingo term for land areas above river
levels that remain arid in the dry season although they
are flooded during the rains. In the Gambia, these lands
are higher than the mangrove swamps, but lie below the
levels of the sandstone plateau which is an extension of
the soil type found throughout the southern Senegal and
the Casamance. There are two types of banto faros in
the Gambia--the estuarine and the upper river. The dividing line between the two is found roughly in the vicinity of Kerewan.

BARRA WAR. In 1827, Burungai Sonko, the king of Barra,
disturbed by Commodore Bullen's decision to build a fort
at Barra Point, decided to abrogate the Ceded Mile treaty
of the previous year. This decision resulted in a number
of incidents which culminated in the important Barra War
which did not end until 1831. The hostilities forced Bullen to stop construction on the fort, and for a time it appeared that the British would be driven out of Barra and
the Ceded Mile. At one time the fledgling town of Bathurst was also threatened. The situation was reversed
because the French at Goree dispatched a warship and
troops to aid the British. This aid allowed the British to
recommence construction of Fort Bullen in 1831 which with
its three-gun battery helped to give the British command
of the entrance to the Gambia River.

BARRAKUNDA. A town in the Wuli section of the upper
river area of the Gambia. It was the site of the last of
the upper river factories established by English companies because the falls at Barrakunda marked the limit of
river travel in the dry season. There was a post established there as early as 1651 which was later destroyed
by fire. An English factory was sited there again in 1678
and from time to time traders were posted there as late
as 1810.

BATHURST. The chief city and capital of the Gambia during British administration. It was founded in 1816 by
Alexander Grant, who had purchased the island of Banjul
from the King of Kombo. Grant renamed the island St.
Mary's and named the town in honor of the then Secretary
of State for Colonies, Lord Henry Bathurst. The streets
were laid out in a modified grid pattern and named after
the chief leaders during the recent war with Napoleon.
The name of the town was changed in 1973 to Banjul by
the independent Gambian government. The population in
1985 was estimated to be in excess of 50,000 persons. See
also BANJUL.

BATHURST, LORD HENRY. British Secretary of State for
Colonies from 1812-1828. Captain Alexander Grant in
1816 named his new town on St. Mary's Island in honor
of Bathurst who had authorized the project to restore
British prestige on the Gambia River.

BATTIMANSA. Described by Cadamosto in 1456 as the Mandingo ruler of a portion of the north bank approximately
sixty miles from the mouth of the Gambia River (probably
Baddibu). Battimansa received the Europeans in a very
friendly fashion and treated them as honored guests during their 11-day stay, traded with them, and then signed
a treaty of friendship.

BINTANG. A village located approximately five miles up the
Bintang Bolon from Bintang Point. It was the residence
of the king of Foni and was one of the most important
trade locales in the 18th century. Both the English and
French maintained factories there in the century after
1685. English independent traders continued to use Bintang as a trading base in the early 19th century.

BINTANG BOLON (creek).   An important feature noted by
    early European visitors to the Gambia.   It rises south of
    Elephant Island, north of the watershed of the Casamance
    River, and flows westward for approximately eighty miles
    before joining the Gambia River at Bintang Point some
    thirty miles from St. Mary's Island.   It formed the divid-
    ing line between Kiang and Foni.   From the earliest peri-
    od of European activity there were always a number of
    temporary trading stations located along the Bolon.   The
    Royal African Company maintained a major trade factory at
    Bintang.   In some early literature, the stream is referred
    to as the Geregia River.

BLACKBURNE, SIR KENNETH W.   An official of the Colonial
    Service in the West Indies, seconded to the Gambia to
    head a five-man development committee appointed by Gov-
    ernor Southorn in 1940.   This committee was the Gambia's
    response to a Colonial Office directive that all colonies
    and territories prepare detailed analyses of the needs of
    the separate segments of the Empire and make recommen-
    dations for use of Colonial Development and Welfare Funds
    at the conclusion of World War II.   The Blackburne Report
    issued in 1943 was the first logical statement of the Gam-
    bia's needs which encompassed all areas of the economy.
    The report, although many of its recommendations were
    ignored, served as the guide for Gambian development
    between 1945-1950.

BLOOD, SIR HILARY.   Governor of the Gambia during the
    latter stages of World War II and immediately afterward,
    from 1942-1947.   His administration was responsible for
    drawing up proposals for the improvements of the Colony
    area utilizing Colonial Development and Welfare Funds.
    Although these funds fell short of expectations, the mod-
    ernization of the water supply, the sewage system, paved
    streets and improvements of the port date to Blood's ad-
    ministration.   Later Sir Hilary became governor of Malta
    and was the director of the United Nations-sponsored
    plebiscite in the British Cameroon.

BOJANG, TOMANI.   The last Soninke king of the Kombo.
    After being hard pressed by the Marabout dissidents at
    Gunjur in 1863-64, he agreed to the truce with Fodi Kabba
    and Fodi Silla arranged by Governor D'Arcy.   For over

half a decade there was relative peace between the two
factions in Kombo, broken only by sporadic violence. In
1870, Tomani Bojang, upon learning of the proposed cession of British territories to the French, addressed a dig-
nified note to the Queen requesting that if she no longer
wanted those areas deeded to her that she could "return
my territory back to me as an act of friendship."   The
British government informed him that it could not accede
to his request. In the troubled years of the 1870s neither
could the British protect him completely from his Marabout
enemies who had become even more powerful. Hostilities
broke out in 1871, and within two years all of the Soninke
towns in Kombo with the exception of Busumballa and
Brikama were in Soninke hands. In the following year,
Bojang lost Brikama, and a small remnant of his territory
was saved only by a British arranged truce in 1874. In
the following year, Fodi Silla began the war again and his
forces took Busumballa, forcing the king to take refuge at
Lamin, within a few yards of British territory. The British Administrator, fearing that war would spread to British Kombo, warned Tomani Bojang not to expect any
British aid. The king, therefore, was forced to accept
Fodi Silla's humiliating terms. He shaved his head, became a Muslim, and tore down his stockade. His old enemy then allowed him enough land for himself and his people, in the territory which Bojang's dynasty had ruled
for over two centuries.

BOOKER, JOHN. Chief agent of the Royal African Company
in the Gambia from 1688 until his death in mid-1693. He
was one of the most loyal and successful of the company
servants in Africa. The outbreak of the war with France
in 1689 found him in charge of fewer than 200 men and no
ships of war permanently stationed on the river. Nevertheless, he used visiting company vessels to drive French
shipping from the coast, to deal with privateers, and finally to transport an expeditionary force against St. Louis
and Goree. Both French stations were captured in December 1692, their stores seized, and their defenses demol-
ished. His death by fever removed the one company man
who might have resisted the French forces which recaptured St. Louis and Goree in 1693.

BRAVO, MAJOR ALEXANDER. Acting Administrator of the
Gambia in 1870 who attempted to rebut the arguments of

local and British merchants against the exchange of the
Gambia for suitable French territory elsewhere.

BRIDGES, PHILIP R. Civil servant and solicitor, born in
England in 1922. He was educated at Aberdeen University and served with the Royal Artillery attached to the
West African Frontier Force in Burma during World War II.
He was posted to the Gambia in 1954 as solicitor to the
Supreme Court and later served in the Attorney-General's
office. In 1964 he was appointed Attorney-General, a
post he continued to hold after independence, being the
only European in the Gambia's Ministry.

BRITISH WEST AFRICAN SETTLEMENTS. Until 1843, the
administration of Sierra Leone and the Gambia was the
primary responsibility of a governor resident at Freetown.
The Gambia was administered directly by an Administrator
subordinate to his chief in Sierra Leone. In 1843 the administration of each territory became the province of a
governor resident in each locale, and thus the Gambia
was severed from direct connection with Sierra Leone.
One of the major results of the Parliamentary investiga-
tions of 1865 was to return to the older system, placing
all the British territories--Sierra Leone, Gambia, the Gold
Coast, and Lagos--under one governor with overall responsibility. Thus the administration of the Gambia became subordinate to decisions made in Freetown. In 1874 the British possessions on the Gold Coast and at Lagos were separated from Sierra Leone, but the Gambia remained under
the control of the governor of the British West African
Settlements. It was not until November 1888 that the Gambia was released from this cumbersome and economically
debilitating dependence, and it became a separate Colony.

BROWN, THOMAS. British merchant whose firm was one of
the largest in the Gambia in the late 1860s and early 1870s.
Brown and Company had been trading in the hinterland
since the early 1830s and Brown had made enough money
to retire to England in 1854. However, five years later
he was back and soon his agents were challenging French
firms for supremacy on the lower Gambia River. He was
a member of the Legislative Council during much of that
period of early negotiations with France over exchanging
the Gambia. He was one of the chief opponents to both
attempts by Britain to be rid of the Gambia. He wrote

long polemical letters, signed memorials, and personally
lobbied at the Colonial Office against the trade since he
was convinced that British and African firms would not
receive adequate compensation and would be forced out
of business by the French. Brown and Company continued in operation until 1880 and Brown was the last of the
pioneer British merchants to continue to reside in Bathurst.

BRUE, ANDRE. Director-General of the French Senegal
Company after 1697, with his headquarters at St. Louis.
He was dedicated to driving English traders from the Senegambia and gaining French dominance of trade on the Gambia River. However, he was not able to accomplish this
despite a quarter of a century of effort directed toward
this end. Major reasons for his failure were his inability
to control piracy, the losses sustained by the Senegal
Company during the War of Spanish Succession, and the
growing economic weaknesses of the Company.

BULLEN, CHARLES. A Commodore in the British Navy and
a veteran of Trafalgar who in 1826 was in command of
HMS Maidstone which arrived in the Gambia to support
the acting Governor of Sierra Leone, Kenneth MacAulay,
in his negotiations with Burungai Sonko, the king of
Barra. Subsequently a treaty was signed ceding to
Britain the whole right bank of the river one mile inland
from Jinnak Creek to Jokadu Creek. Immediately after
the signing, Commodore Bullen transported two cannons to
Barra Point. A military guard was placed over these
guns and the site was named Fort Bullen in honor of the
Commodore.

BUR. The title of the king in the Serer states of Sine and
Saloum.

BURBA. The title given to the king in the earliest dominant
Wolof state of Jolof.

BURTON, SIR RICHARD. A distinguished 19th-century explorer, translator, and author. As British Consul to
Fernando Po, he visited the Gambia in 1863 and left his
impressions of Bathurst and the British government in a
book, Wanderings in West Africa from Liverpool to Fernando Po, under the pseudonymous initials F.R.G.S.

BUSUMBULLA.   A town in Kombo midway between Sukuta
    and Brikama which was the main fortified base of the
    rulers.   By mid-1874, Busumbulla was the only town loyal
    to the Soninke king, Tomani Bojang.   Its capture in the
    following year forced him to capitulate and accept Islam
    in exchange for the right to continue to live in Kombo.

-C-

CD&W   see   COLONIAL DEVELOPMENT AND WELFARE ACTS

CDC   see   COLONIAL DEVELOPMENT CORPORATION

CADAMOSTO, ALVISE DA.   A Venetian captain employed by
    Prince Henry of Portugal, commissioned in 1455 to investi-
    gate rumors of lands along the Gambia River where great
    quantities of gold could be obtained.   Sailing in a 90-ton
    ship, he was joined off Cape Verde by Antoniotto Usidi-
    mare with two ships, and together they entered the estu-
    ary of the Gambia River.   Armed resistance from Africans
    in canoes so unnerved the crews that they refused to pro-
    ceed further.   In the following year, Cadamosto returned
    with three ships to the Gambia and proceeded approximate-
    ly sixty miles upriver.   He was warmly received by the
    Mandingo ruler of Baddibu, concluded a treaty of friend-
    ship with him, and acquired a few slaves and some gold
    in their trading.   After staying in Baddibu for 11 days,
    he sailed down river, explored the southern coastline as
    far as the Casamance River, and then returned to Portu-
    gal.

CADI (QADI, XADI).   Arabic term for a judge.   Sometimes
    reserved for the supreme judge or leader of an Islamic
    community.

CAMARA, ANDREW DAVID.   A politician, born at Mansajang
    in the upper river region in 1923.   He is a Fulbe convert
    to Christianity and was educated in the Protectorate and
    Bathurst.   He was a teacher for 10 years before entering
    politics in 1958.   Camara was elected in 1960 as an Inde-
    pendent member of the House of Assembly.   He shifted to
    the United Party and served as minister when P. S. N'Jie
    was Chief Minister.   In 1962, he again changed his party

affiliation to the PPP and was returned to the House with a large majority. He was named Minister of Education in 1963 and held that position for many years. He was appointed Minister of External Affairs to succeed A. B. N'Jie, a post which he continued to hold in 1973.

CAMERON, SIR EDWARD J. Governor of the Gambia during World War I, serving from 1914 to 1920. He was responsible for putting into effect the provisions of the Comprehensive Protectorate Ordinance of 1913. In 1919, he issued another Protectorate Ordinance which further defined relative powers of the central government and the chiefs, and also introduced a new scale of Protectorate taxes. It was during Cameron's tenure of office that British firms gained supremacy in trade from their French competitors. The failure of Cameron and his successor, C. H. Armitage, to act quickly to equalize the exchange rate for the five franc piece eventually cost the Gambia over ₤200,000.

CARTER, SIR GILBERT. Administrator of the Gambia from 1888 to 1891. During his short term of office, Britain reversed its decades old policy against territorial expansion. In 1888, Carter was ordered to enter into definite treaties of cession with Gambian chiefs. His recommendation to his superiors that they claim a large segment of the hinterland of the Gambia River was largely ignored by the delegates to the Paris Conference in 1889. After the declaration of the Protectorate, Carter with his small force and few resources could do little but announce the change to the upper and middle river Gambian chiefs.

CASAMANCE. A small area lying between the Gambia and Guinea Bissau. It is one of the seven administrative regions of the Republic of Senegal, almost completely separated from the rest of the state by the Gambia. The upper and middle portions of the territory belong to the Sahel zone while the lower Casamance marks the beginning of the West African rain forest zone. Inhabited by Papel, Balante, Tucolor, Fulbe, and Mandingo, the present day Casamance was historically a part of the Gambia River complex and it was not until 1889 that it was arbitrarily separated from the Gambia.

CEDED MILE. In June 1826, Kenneth MacAulay, acting Governor of Sierra Leone, negotiated with Burungai

Sonko, the king of Barra, the cession to the Crown of a
coastal strip, one mile in depth beginning at Jinnak Creek
on the west as far as Jokadu Creek to the east. In January 1832, following the Barra War, this cession was re-
confirmed and the area controlled by the British was extended slightly. The Ceded Mile was administered by the
British as a part of the Colony, even after the declaration
of a Protectorate over the hinterland areas in 1889.

CHAM, MAMADOU CADIJA. A civil servant and politician,
  born at Basse on August 19, 1938, and educated at St.
  Georges Primary School, Basse and St. Augustine's Secondary School, Bathurst. Entered civil service in 1958
  and served four years until elected member of Parliament
  for Tumana, in 1962 and 1965 as a member of the United
  Party. Joined the PPP and was reelected to Parliament.
  Appointed Minister of Education, Youth and Sports and
  later served as Minister of Trade and Finance until the
  cabinet reshuffle of 1981.

CHOWN, THOMAS, SR. British merchant who formed a
  family-owned trading company which operated in the Gambia from the early 1830s. He combined his efforts with
  those of other British merchants such as T. F. Quin and
  Thomas Brown, and Gambian traders like J. D. Cole and
  E. J. Nicol to oppose the 1866-1870 plan to cede the Gambia to France.

CHOWN, THOMAS, JR. British merchant who had taken
  control of the family business interests in the Gambia in
  1870. He was one of the ten members of the Gambia Committee which lobbied successfully in 1875 and 1876 against
  the revived plan of the Colonial Office to exchange the
  Gambia for French territory.

CHRISTENSEN, ERIC HERBERT. A civil servant, born Octo-
  ber 29, 1923 in Bathurst. Educated at St. Augustine's
  Secondary School. Teacher at St. Augustine's 1941-43.
  Military service 1944-45; clerk in Secretariat 1946-47;
  served as Vice-Consul French Consulate, 1947-60; Attache
  Senegalese Consulate General 1961-65; Assistant Secretary,
  External Affairs in Gambia Government, 1965-66; Assistant
  Secretary, Prime Minister's Office, 1966-67; Head of Civil
  Service 1967. Awarded CMG, 1968.

CHURCH OF ENGLAND. Its activities in the Gambia date
from 1821 when at the request of Sir Charles MacCarthy,
a chaplain was sent for the Bathurst garrison. However,
due to the high mortality rate, there was normally no
Anglican representative in Bathurst during the first half
of the 19th century. In 1836, the government allowed
Anglicans to use the former officers' mess for church
services. No permanent church in Bathurst was erected
until the present structure was built in 1901. In 1855,
missionary work was begun by the Anglican Church of
the West Indies among the Susus along the Rio Pongas.
In 1935, this area was combined with that of the Gambia
and the first Bishop for this new diocese was appointed.
Although not as active in the education field as the Wesleyans, the Anglicans did open a church school in Bathurst as early as 1869 and maintained from the 1920s one
small elementary school in the Protectorate.

CISSE, BIRAM. Born into an important Marabout family at
Kaur, he early came under the influence of Ma Bâ and
proved himself one of the better military leaders of the
kingdom of Rip. After Ma Bâ's death, he precipitated a
rebellion against Momadou N'Dare Bâ by refusing to dis-
mantle his fortifications at Kaur. He was aided in his
struggle against Momadou by Musa Molloh and by the Bur
Saloum, Guedel M'Bodj. By the early 1880s, Cisse had
managed to drive Momadou from most of the vast territory he had once controlled. Complications arose, however, when Saër Maty, the son of Ma Bâ, claimed the
throne of Baddibu and Cisse found this new enemy more
formidable than Momadou. Despite considerable military
success, particularly in the campaign of 1885, he was unable to completely defeat Saër Maty, and in 1886, agreed
to the proposal of British mediators to accept Saër Maty
as his suzerain provided he could keep his territory and
receive a stipend from the British. When the latter was
not forthcoming, Cisse refused the agreement. In the civil
war, both parties had encroached on the territory of Saloum and the French, fearing a recurrence of Rip domination there, sent a military column against Saër Maty in
1887, defeated his armies, and forced him to flee. Cisse
was not involved directly in this action and received from
the French guarantees of a part of the kingdom of Rip.
However, after rumors of an impending renewal of violence
reached him, the French Commandant at Nioro arrested
Cisse in June 1888 and he was exiled to Gabon.

CLOSER ASSOCIATION WITH SENEGAL. Relates to the official attempts and private views concerned with political,
social, and economic reunification of the Senegambia.
Serious consideration was given to this question by the
British even before the constitutional advances of the
1960s. The British and Senegalese did not want to appear to force Gambia into an unwanted association, but
rejoining the two areas seemed an obvious solution to the
economic non-viability of the Gambia, and it would rectify
the arbitrary division established by the Anglo-French
Convention of 1889. In 1961, an interministerial committee was created by President Senghor and P. S. N'Jie to
examine ways toward a practical union of the two polities.
A United Nations report favored some form of ultimate political union in order to raise the economic level of both
countries. The public statements of the leaders of France,
Britain, and Senegal indicated their approval of closer
association. A treaty of association between Senegal and
Gambia was also signed in the early 1960s. Little was
done during the next 15 years to achieve meaningful political association. There were regular meetings of the
interministerial committee and each state agreed to coop-
erate on certain economic developments most of which were
beyond the capacity of either party. The PPP leadership
feared that in any scheme the Gambia would be dominated
by the larger French-speaking Senegalese government.
The improvement of Gambia's economic prospects also
made closer association less of a desirable goal. Continued smuggling from the Gambia and a number of border
violations by Senegal appeared to show that closer association was largely a facade. The coup attempt of July
1981 aimed at unseating President Jawara and the PPP
changed the climate of opinion. Jawara invoked the mutual defense treaty and Senegal sent in troops which
quelled the uprising. Relatively defenseless and needing
continued Senegalese military support, Jawara and the
Gambian legislature late in 1981 approved an agreement
which created the Confederation of Senegambia. This
treaty formed a joint executive with the Abdou Diouf as
President and Jawara as Vice-President, and planned for
the ultimate establishment of a joint legislature. As the
events of 1981 faded, the Gambia government has been
less than enthusiastic about speeding up the process of
association. All of the old arguments against a functioning federation of the two states reemerged and politicians

in both states began to make recriminations reminiscent of
the 1970s. See also CONFEDERATION OF SENEGAMBIA.

COLONIAL DEVELOPMENT AND WELFARE ACTS (CD&W).
The first of these acts was passed by the British Parliament in early 1940 and represented a reversal of the previous doctrine for the Dependent Empire. Instead of de-
manding fiscal self-sufficiency of all territories, Parliament
recognized a responsibility to aid in developing all of its
territories even though an area might not itself have the
available funds. Under these acts, Britain, although hard-
pressed in the years immediately after World War II, made
massive grants of funds to its African territories. Although falling far short of expectations, the Gambia in
the decade after 1957 received over Ł1½ million from Colonial Development and Welfare funds. These funded the
construction of a new bridge, a high school, Victoria
Hospital, and a better water supply, paved streets, and
an adequate drainage system for the capital city. The
bulk of the funds allocated for the Protectorate went for
the improvement of agriculture and building an asphalt
road from Brikama to Mansa Konko and construction of
the hospital at Bansang.

COLONIAL DEVELOPMENT CORPORATION (CDC). Created
by the British government in 1948 to devise development
schemes which would secure the dual purpose of providing necessary income for the territories and also a profit
for the corporation. The direction of the corporation was
the responsibility of a Board of Directors of eight members with Lord Trefgarne as chairman. The corporation
was concerned with funding two major projects in the
Gambia. The first was a large-scale mechanized project
to clear land, plant, and harvest rice mechanically on
4,700 acres of land near Wallikunda. The project was
not successful and after the expenditure of great sums,
the facilities were taken over in 1953 by the Gambian
government which continued to operate the farm as an
experimental station. The other project of the corporation
in the Gambia was even more expensive and glaringly unsuccessful. From 1948 to early 1951, the corporation ex-
pended nearly one million pounds in the Yundum egg
scheme. A combination of factors--poor management,
over optimistic estimates of profits, failure to confer
with local officials, and chicken disease--combined to

make the Yundum project one of the corporation's greatest African failures.

COMPANY OF MERCHANTS TRADING TO AFRICA (British).
Created by an act of Parliament in 1750, it was the successor to the bankrupt Royal African Company which, however, was not divested of all its powers until 1752. The Company of Merchants was prohibited from all trading in its corporate capacity. It was directed by an appointed executive committee empowered to make rules regarding trading in West Africa and which thus could charge trading fees and customs duties. It received an annual subsidy from Parliament for the maintenance of the trading forts and stations. The Crown exercised supervisory control over the activities of the company. The fort on James Island was repaired and restaffed, and with the aid of ships of the British navy, French attempts to dominate Gambian trade from Albreda were thwarted even before the outbreak of the Seven Years War. During that war, the British beat off a French attack on James Island in 1757, and in the following year captured and garrisoned all the main French bases in Senegal. At the outbreak of the war, the company had relinquished its rights of administration. Its territories were administered by the military until 1765 when the Colony of the Senegambia was created with its centrum at St. Louis. During the War for American Independence, a French force reoccupied St. Louis and razed James Fort in early 1779. The Treaty of Versailles of 1783 restored to the French all they had lost in the Senegambia, and in the same year the Crown turned over to the Company of Merchants control over the Gambia area. The company showed no great zeal in reestablishing trade relations. Parliament many times refused a grant which the company directors felt necessary for the reconstruction of James Fort, and it was never rebuilt. British trade on the river was maintained by private merchants. Finally in 1816, the Crown decided to send Captain Alexander Grant with a small party to build a fort near the river's mouth whose main function would be to control the slave trade. The Company of Merchants did not underwrite this venture, and there developed in theory, a duality of control, Finally in 1821, all the forts and territories were taken from the company and placed under the direct jurisdiction of the Crown.

CONFEDERATION OF SENEGAMBIA. One of the factors that led
    Great Britain to agree so readily to Gambian independence
    was the belief that this would lead rapidly to an amalga-
    mation of Gambia and Senegal. Continued prosperity dur-
    ing the 1960s meant that such a closer association appeared
    less attractive to Gambians who feared losing their free-
    dom of action to the more populous French-speaking Sene-
    gal. The abortive coup attempt in July 1981 against Pres-
    ident Jawara's government changed the official attitude.
    Jawara was restored to power only with assistance from
    Senegal. Needing continued military support, the Presi-
    dent and his government entered into an agreement in
    December 1981 creating the Confederation of the Sene-
    gambia. By this agreement both states pledged continued
    consultation and cooperation on economic and foreign pol-
    icy in the near future. Further, it created the theoreti-
    cal infrastructure for a future single government for both
    areas.

    The President of Senegal became the President of this
    new polity while the Gambian leader assumed the position
    of Vice President. A common federal legislature would be
    created at some future date. The agreement promised
    that both existing states would recognize and protect
    within a federal structure the uniqueness of both soci-
    eties. In the four years following the agreement there
    have been protocols signed on common defense policies,
    external relations, communications, and information. Such
    important areas as monetary and general economic cooper-
    ation to establish a free trade area between the states
    was still under consideration in 1986. A gendarmerie
    equipped by France and trained by Senegalese officers
    was formed in early 1986 to replace the Gambia Field
    Force, which had been disbanded after the attempted
    coup. Jealousy over national uniqueness and fears of
    being dominated by Senegal remain potent divisive fac-
    tors preventing the quick implementation of closer politi-
    cal union. See also CLOSER ASSOCIATION WITH SENE-
    GAL.

CONFERENCE OF PROTECTORATE CHIEFS. An annual
    meeting of the seyfolu of the Gambia was instituted in
    1944 as a means of better communication with the gover-
    nor and the central agencies of the administration. The
    conferences which were held at different locales each
    year were occasions of great pomp and ceremony. The

meetings all followed a similar format. The governor
would address the chiefs, outlining his proposals for action for the coming year. This would be followed by
presentations by the heads of the central departments of
their activities during the previous year and their plans
for the coming year. Until 1958, the chiefs did not take
an active role, asked few questions, and accepted the
government's predetermined policy without demur. From
1958 onward, a number of chiefs, at times vehemently,
began to comment and question the performance of the
government. However, political parties soon supplanted
the chiefs as the dominant spokesmen for the Protectorate
and the conference never became more than a passive
sounding board for the central administration.

CONTON, WILLIAM. Novelist and educator, born in 1925 in
    Bathurst where his father was a clergyman. He was edu-
    cated in the Gambia and Sierra Leone before leaving for
    university training at Durham in England. After receiv-
    ing his B.A., he returned to West Africa where he be-
    came the principal of the Government Secondary School
    at Bo in Sierra Leone. He is the author of The African,
    published in 1960, one of the first novels by an African
    to gain worldwide circulation and acclaim.

COURLAND, DUCHY OF. An independent Baltic Duchy in
    the 17th century under the suzerainty of the kings of
    Poland. James, Duke of Courland, caught up in mercan-
    tilistic dreams of the wealth of Guinea, formed a trading
    company in 1650. In the following year his agents leased
    Banjul from the king of Kombo, a small plot of land at
    Juffure on the north bank, and most important, an island
    in the Gambia River from the king of Barra. The island
    was named St. Andrews (later renamed James Island by
    the British). The company sent a group of settlers under
    Major Fock who built an excellent fort on the island from
    whence the Courlanders hoped to dominate the river trade.
    The Duke's dream of a mercantile empire based on the
    Gambia and the West Indies were dashed by the corrup-
    tion of his lieutenants and the open hostility of greater
    European powers and the events in the Baltic. The Duke
    was captured by Charles X of Sweden in 1658 and he as-
    signed the rights to manage his Gambian holdings to the
    Dutch West Indies Company. In 1661, St. Andrews Island
    was captured by the English under Major Robert Holmes.

In 1664, Courland ceded its rights in the Gambia to England in return for a guarantee to respect the Duke's control over Tobago in the West Indies.

-D-

DCA   see   DEMOCRATIC CONGRESS ALLIANCE

DP   see   DEMOCRATIC PARTY

DABO, DARI BANA. The Marabout chief of Sankandi and a
    follower of Fodi Kabba in the late 1890s. When the long-
    standing quarrel over rice lands with the Soninkes of
    Jataba became critical, Travelling Commissioner F. C. Sit-
    well investigated and awarded the lands to Jataba. Dari
    Bana Dabo refused to be bound by this decision and de-
    cided to fight when Sitwell, accompanied by Commissioner
    Silva and 11 African constables, appeared at Sankandi in
    early 1900 to enforce the award. In the ensuing skirmish,
    the two Travelling Commissioners, a neighboring chief,
    and six constables were killed. As soon as troops were
    available, the British in conjunction with the French
    moved to pacify those areas loyal to Fodi Kabba. French
    troops moved on Medina, Fodi Kabba's stronghold, in March
    1901. The British allied with Musa Molloh had already taken
    Sankandi in January. Dari Bana Dabo fled to French ter-
    ritory where he was captured and turned over to the
    British for trial. He and two of his lieutenants were
    tried before the Supreme Court in Bathurst and found
    guilty of the deaths of Sitwell and his party. Dari Bana
    Dabo was sentenced to death and executed.

DARBO, BAKARY BUNJA. Civil servant and politician, born
    at Dumbutto, Lower River Division, in 1946. He was edu-
    cated at Dumbutto and Kaiaf primary schools and Metho-
    dist Boys High School and received an honors degree in
    modern languages from the University of Ibadan in 1967.
    He received post-graduate training from the University of
    Abidjan, Ivory Coast, and specialized economic training
    from the Bank of America, the National Westminster Bank,
    and Ghana Commercial Bank. He spent two tours in the
    Provincial Administration upriver at Basse and Kerewan;
    the first of these (1967-68) was as Assistant Divisional
    Commissioner, and the second (1970-71) as Divisional

Commissioner. Between these he served as Assistant
Secretary in the Ministry of External Affairs. In July
1971 he was appointed Director of Economic and Technical
Affairs and three years later was made Manager of the
commercial operations of the Gambia Commercial and Development Bank in Banjul. In 1979 he was appointed
Gambian High Commissioner to the Republic of Senegal, a
position he held until September 1981, when he was nominated a member of Parliament and given the post of Minister of Information and Tourism. He was elevated to
Vice President of the Gambia in May 1982.

D'ARCY, G. A. K. (Colonel). Succeeded Lieutenant-Colonel
O'Connor as Governor of the Gambia in 1859. He arrived
in the midst of a yellow fever epidemic which had reduced
the European population of Bathurst to fewer than a dozen
persons. His pleas to the Colonial Office for extra funds
to be able to drain Half Die and improve the sanitation
facilities of the Colony fell on deaf ears and many of his
recommendations were not carried into effect a half-century
later. D'Arcy's expedition against Baddibu in 1861 set in
motion the series of events which brought Ma Bâ to power.
Throughout his tenure, D'Arcy was constrained from any
policy toward Ma Bâ and the middle and upper river areas
which would have committed the British government to
any more expense. The treaty of friendship D'Arcy
signed with Ma Bâ in February 1863 concerning Niumi
was a good example of the type of intervention D'Arcy
was limited to. Although some of Ma Bâ's lieutenants
continued to cause trouble in Niumi, Ma Bâ kept his word
and did not again disturb the area. In the Kombos,
D'Arcy had the force to confront the Marabouts and Fodi
Kabba, and to maintain an uneasy status quo through
1864 and 1865. The chief disturber of the peace was
Amer Faal who raided into the Ceded Mile. In July 1866,
with naval support and 500 reinforcements from Essau,
D'Arcy's West Indian troops stormed Tubab Kolon, Amer
Faal's strongpoint. D'Arcy's ideas concerning British influence in the Senegambia were reflected in the report of
Colonel St. George Ord in 1865, but aside from a few
punitive forays such as Tubab Kolon, D'Arcy could do
little to increase British control along the river.

DE JASPAS, MELCHOIR. An Armenian resident of Great
Britain who was used by the Royal African Company to

translate some of Job ben Solomon's Arabic letters. The
company decided to use his language skills and sent him
to the Gambia in 1737. Because of maltreatment, he left
the company in the following year. However, in 1740 he
was reemployed and accompanied Job ben Solomon to Bondu. In 1744 he journeyed overland to Cachau in Portuguese Guinea. Little of concrete trading value was obtained for the company by de Jaspas in his explorations,
perhaps because the outbreak of war with France in 1743
focused the company's attention elsewhere.

DEMA. Wolof term for witches, whom they fear greatly. A
person becomes a dema through his mother. If the mother
is a witch, then the children are also suspected of being
able to do great harm. Witches are believed to be able
to take animal or bird form and to eat people's souls and
drink their blood.

DEMOCRATIC CONGRESS ALLIANCE (DCA). Formed in 1960
by a merger of the Democratic Party and the Muslim Congress because the leaders of the older parties, Reverend
J. C. Faye and I. M. Garba-Jahumpa, wanted a stronger,
Protectorate-wide party to contest the elections against
the United Party and the People's Progressive Party.
However, only three of their candidates were elected to
the House of Representatives in 1960. In 1961 the DCA
leaders reached an agreement with Jawara and the PPP,
and although there was no merger, the DCA cooperated
with the PPP for the elections of 1962. Despite the victory of the PPP, the DCA could win only one seat in the
expanded House of Representatives. This failure and differences of political philosophy between Garba-Jahumpa
and Faye soon led to the breakup of the DCA.

DEMOCRATIC PARTY (DP). The First political party in the
Gambia. It was formed in February 1951, by the adherents of Reverend John C. Faye to contest for one of the
Bathurst seats in the Legislative Council under the provisions of the Constitution of that year. It was successful
in returning Reverend Faye to office. In the 1950s, this
Colony based party was the vehicle by which Reverend
Faye successfully opposed his political rivals, I. M. Garba-
Jahumpa and P. S. N'Jie. However, Faye came to be considered by his constituents as a tool of the Britich colonial
regime. This factor and the extension of the elections to

the Protectorate in 1960 deeply undercut the influence of
the Democratic Party. Prior to the elections of 1960, it
was merged with the Muslim Congress to form the Democratic Congress Alliance. The failure of this coalition in
the two elections of 1960 and 1962 resulted in strains between the leaders, and I. M. Garba-Jahumpa withdrew
and reconstituted the Muslim Congress. Many of Reverend Faye's adherents shifted their allegiance to either the
People's Progressive Party or the United Party, and the
Democratic Party was not revived.

DEMONETIZATION. The crisis over the exchange of the
five franc piece in the Gambia after World War I caused
the British government in January 1922 to redeem all
those coins then in circulation at the legal rate. The
legal rate in the Gambia was approximately 1-3/4 times
the world rate. Failure of the government to act soon
caused the demonetization to cost over £2,000,000 more
than if these coins had been redeemed at the world rate.
The cost of demonetization was borne by the poor government of the Gambia.

DENTON, SIR GEORGE C. The first chief executive of the
modern era in the Gambia to be commissioned by the Colonial Office as Governor instead of Administrator. He
completed the work begun by his successor, Sir R. B.
Llewellyn, in devising the framework of British rule in
the Protectorate. This was done by a series of Protectorate Ordinances which refined and clarified the earlier
system. The most important of these Ordinances was that
of 1902 and two modifying ones in 1909. Denton's main
contribution to the Gambia was his resistance to the requirements of the Anglo-British Convention of 1904 which
would have assigned a mid-river port on the Gambia River
to the French. His arguments that such a cession would
destroy the British and Gambian merchants at Bathurst
had considerable influence in determining the dilatory attitude of the Home government in delaying the cession until after World War I when subsequent events made the
French abandon their designs on the middle river areas.
He served as Governor of the Gambia from 1900 to 1911.

DIBBA, SHERIF MUSTAPHA. A politician, born in 1937, the
son of a farmer at Salikini. His father in the early 1960s
became chief of Central Baddibu. Dibba was educated in

government and mission schools and worked briefly as a
clerk for the United Africa Company until he resigned in
1959 to work for the advancement of the People's Progressive Party. He was particularly active in organizing the
youth wing of the party. He was elected to the House of
Assembly in 1960 and returned in all subsequent elections.
In 1964 he became Minister of Labor and in the following
year Minister of Local Government. After the 1966 elections, he was appointed Minister of Works and Communications. After Sherif Sisay was expelled from the PPP,
Dibba was selected to be the Minister of Finance. When
Gambia became a Republic in 1970, he was chosen to be
Vice President while continuing as Finance Minister. He
relinquished the latter portfolio in early 1973 and soon
after was removed as Vice President and demoted to the
less prestigious position of Gambian negotiator to the
European Economic Community. Shortly before the 1977
elections he broke his ties with the PPP and was instrumental in creating a new party, the National Convention
Party (NCP). Although gaining only slightly more than
25 percent of the popular vote for President, his party
captured five seats in the House and became the official
opposition. He was accused of complicity in the 1981
abortive coup in Banjul and was imprisoned for 14 months
before being released by the courts. He campaigned for
the Presidency from his cell and managed to receive over
50,000 votes. But the accusations damaged the NCP and
they were fortunate to retain three seats in the House.
Upon his release, Dibba continued as the major spokesman for the opposition against continued PPP rule.

DIEPPE MERCHANTS. They were the first French traders
to trade openly with Cape Verde, the Gambia, and the
Guinea coast despite Portuguese claims to a monopoly of
trade in all of western Africa. By 1560, they had established regular trade with Cape Verde and in 1570, the
first French ship entered the Gambia River.

DIOUF, ABDOU. President of Senegal from 1980 and of the
Confederation of Senegambia since 1982. He had previ-
ously served as the Prime Minister of Senegal, one of
President Leopold Senghor's most trusted lieutenants
from 1974 to 1980. Diouf was born in 1935 in Louga.
Educated in Senegal and France, he entered the Civil
Service where because of his abilities as an administrator

he was rapidly promoted to senior positions. When Senghor changed the name of Senegal's ruling party and decided to reintroduce the office of Prime Minister, he chose the 38-year-old Diouf, ostensibly because he wanted a man little known throughout the country who would be content to carry out his policies. Diouf, content with his role, has emerged as a dominant political leader since Senghor's retirement. He responded quickly to the Gambia government's pleas for assistance during the abortive attempt in 1981 to overthrow President Jawara. Senegalese troops drove the rebels out of Banjul, restored the legal government, and then maintained order in the damaged capital. Discussions between Diouf and Jawara led the following year to the creation of the confederation. Although more symbolic than actual, the Senegambia accord is perhaps Diouf's greatest success since it could be the foundation for the reunification of the two states.

DIOUF, COUMBA N'DOFFENE. Bur Sine from 1853 to 1871 whose position in the 1860s was threatened from two external forces. The French, following a gradual process of extending their authority into the hinterland, had come to dominate the Wolof states of Baol, Walo, and Cayor to the north. Ma Bâ's armies had conquered much of the north bank kingdoms of the Gambia, Saloum, and Jolof. Sine was thus directly threatened by the raids of Ma Bâ's lieutenants, although for six years Ma Bâ avoided a direct confrontation with the tyeddo of Sine. Coumba N'Doffène resisted French attempts to act as the French cat's paw against Ma Bâ. However, in 1867, Ma Bâ decided to rid himself of the threat of the "pagans" and led a large army into Sine. In one of the most decisive battles in the western Sudan in the 19th century, Coumba N'Doffène's troops defeated the Marabouts, Ma Bâ was killed, and within a short time the threat from a unified interior Islamic kingdom had disappeared. Coumba N'Doffène's later attempts to extend Sine's control over neighboring areas ended tragically with his death by gunshot at Joal in 1871.

DOG ISLAND. A small island located near the right bank of the Gambia River approximately mid-way between Barra Point and Lamin Point. In the 18th century it was called Charles Island by the British. Much of the stone used in the permanent buildings in early day Bathurst was quarried here since the king of Niumi gave Captain Alexander Grant permission to transport stone from Dog Island.

DUMBUYA, FODI KABBA.   A Mandingo Muslim who as a young
man was partly responsible for the beginnings of the
Soninke-Marabout conflict in Kombo. With his power base
at Gunjur, he collaborated with the inhabitants of Sabaji
to attack the Soninke king of Kombo in 1855. The governor, Colonel O'Connor, responded with troops and the
British sustained extremely heavy losses in June of that
year. Although convinced that Fodi Kabba was primarily
responsible for the attack, O'Connor could not retaliate
against him because of the depletion of his force and he
arranged peace between the Marabouts and Soninkes in
the Kombo in April 1856.

   In the next decade, Fodi Kabba and his fellow Marabouts drove out many of the older ruling classes in Kombo, Foni, Kiang, and Jarra. Fodi Kabba and his followers came into conflict with the British once again in 1864
with his attack upon the chief of Yundum. The British
sent a relief column to support that traditional ruler and
the Marabouts were forced to sign another treaty of peace
in 1864. Sometime after this, Fodi Kabba resettled his
family in Fuladu. Whatever the reason for this action, it
frightened Alfa Molloh and his son, Musa, who believed
that Fodi Kabba was attempting to make inroads on their
power in that Fulbe dominated kingdom. Musa attacked
the village and killed or kidnapped the entire family of
Fodi Kabba. The family remnant was released upon the
personal intercession of Governor D'Arcy. However,
Musa's action ushered in a new level of violence along the
south bank which had been relatively free of the maraud-
ing so prevalent in the north bank areas. Fodi Kabba
came to rule over three districts which were isolated from
one another. One was south of Bintang Creek, another
was in western Jarra and eastern Kiang, and the last was
in a part of eastern Jarra. In between these three territories the Soninke managed to maintain a precarious kind
of existence. Fodi Kabba did not attempt to establish a
centralized state such as Ma Bâ had attempted or that
Musa Molloh would create. This failure meant that in the
1870s, raids, looting, and burning were endemic throughout the frontier areas adjacent to Fodi Kabba's territories.
Because of the ill feeling between Fodi Kabba and Musa
Molloh, the land between Jarra and Fuladu was particularly hard hit.

   The division of the Senegambia between France and
Britain in 1889 brought considerable pressure to bear upon

Fodi Kabba. He was viewed by the British as one of the
primary disturbers of the peace and one of the reasons
why the slave trade continued along the southern banks
of the Gambia River. His adherents and those of Fodi
Silla threatened the members of the International Boundary Commission. After this, Fodi Kabba retired to a station in the Casamance, but returned in the following year
to raid the Wolof in Foni.

The British in January 1892 attacked him, destroyed
one of his main stockaded towns, and forced him to retire
again into French territory. From his new base in the
Casamance, he continued to support those Gambians who
were discontented with the new British rule. His adherents would enter British territory, raid villages, take
prisoners, and then recross the border into French territory before any effective pursuit could be organized.
Such raids continued for almost ten years until the murder of Travelling Commissioners Sitwell and Silva at Sankandi in 1900. This town was known to be allied to Fodi
Kabba and the British Colonial authorities decided to destroy his power once and for all. Shortages of troops
due to the South African War postponed the punitive expedition until 1901. The British were joined by the
French, and in a two-pronged attack directed against
Fodi Kabba, Sankandi was taken and Fodi Kabba's territory on the British side was pacified very quickly. The
second phase of the campaign was carried out directly
against the main Marabout force, and in March 1901, his
fortified town of Medina was taken and Fodi Kabba was
killed. This action brought to an end a 50-year career
which spanned the entirety of the Soninke-Marabout Wars
in the Senegambia.

DUTCH WEST INDIES COMPANY see WEST INDIES COMPA-
NY (DUTCH)

                              -E-

ELEPHANT ISLAND. A large island located approximately
100 miles from the ocean at approximately 15° 20' longi-
tude where the Gambia River begins a great bend to the
north. It briefly divides the river into two channels.
Above Elephant Island the water is normally not saline.

EROPINA. One of the nine Mandingo kingdoms located along
the south bank of the Gambia River. Eropina was one of
the smaller polities located opposite Deer Island. During
the Soninke-Marabout Wars, it was conquered by Alfa Molloh and incorporated into his kingdom of Fuladu. In the
20th century reorganization of the Protectorate, the area
which was Eropina was joined to the old kingdom of Niamina and this composite was divided into three segments
each under the direction of a chief.

EXECUTIVE COUNCIL. One of the two councils utilized in
British colonies to assist the governor in making decisions.
From 1843 to 1866, the Gambia had a small nominated Executive Council. There was no council during the period
from 1866 until the nominated council was reconstituted in
1888. The official or government appointees constituted a
majority. No provision was made for members of the Executive Council to be responsible to a legislative unit, and
it remained advisory until being phased out by the new
constitutional instruments just prior to independence.

-F-

FACTOR. An agent of a Chartered Company who was given
the responsibility for disposing of trade goods for the
company. The chief factors for most of the British companies in the Gambia also were held responsible for ad-
ministering James Fort and the outlying trading stations,
and applying the common law to all Europeans in their
jurisdiction. Although the position was primarily commercial, many factors, particularly during the century-long
rivalry between France and Britain, were forced to assume military command as well.

FAIDHERBE, GENERAL LOUIS L. C. Governor of Senegal
from 1854-1861 and from 1863-1865. He was one of the
designers of the early French forward policy in West Africa. In his first term, he improved the economic structure of the small colony, constructed an efficient small
African army, defeated the southern Mauritanian sheikhs,
and sponsored the activities of French merchants in the.
peanut producing areas of Cayor, Sine, and Saloum. It
was Faidherbe's newfound strength which checked the
westward movement of Al Hajj Umar in the middle Senegal

River region. By pressing for the building of a telegraph
line to link St. Louis to Dakar, he committed France to a
policy of interference in Cayor and Baol, and by construct-
ing forts in the Serer states, extended French influence
almost to the banks of the Gambia River. Faidherbe and
his successors in the 1860s followed a shifting policy of
diplomacy and power in helping to check the expansionist
activities of Ma Bâ. The defeat of Ma Bâ at the Somb by
the Sine tyeddo represented a vindication of French policy and laid the groundwork for eventual French expansion into the deep hinterland of the Senegambia.

FANAL. The Portuguese word meaning a lighthouse or lan-
tern, but which today refers to the building of lightweight
wood and paper model ships by differing Muslim and Christian societies. These highly detailed ships are lighted by
candles and are the focal point for a major celebration and
parade through all the major streets of Banjul on Christ-
mas Eve.

FARABANNA. The eldest son of the appropriate lineage in
the 19th-century state of Wuli. He had greater political
influence than king's sons in other Mandingo states and
lived in a separate fortified compound in the chief town.

FAYE, JOHN COLLEY. Educator, minister, and politician,
born in Bathurst in 1908. He was educated at St. Mary's
Anglican School and the Methodist Boys High School. He
received a first class teacher's certificate in 1927 and became a tutor at the Methodist Boys High School. From
1932-34 he was headmaster of Methodist Central School
before transferring to St. Mary's Anglican School where
he became headmaster in 1938. Four years later he became the headmaster of Krista Kunda School in the Protectorate and held this position until 1948. In 1947, he became a deacon of the Anglican Commission and received
an M.B.E. for his pioneering work in education. He was
elected to the Bathurst Town Council first in 1940, and
returned three times unopposed before his posting upriver.
From November 1947 to February 1951, he represented
the upper river area as a nominated member of the Legislative Council. In February 1951, he was instrumental in
creating the Democratic Party, the first political party in
the Gambia, and was elected to the Legislative Council at
the head of the poll. In the subsequent elections in the

1950s, Faye was reelected to the Council and served until June 1960. From 1954 until 1960, he served as ministerial head of Works and Communications. In 1960, Faye joined the Democratic Party with the Muslim Congress Party of I. M. Garba-Jahumpa to form the Democratic Congress Alliance. Despite this merger, Faye was defeated for election to the House of Assembly. He was leader of the DCA until 1963 when Garba-Jahumpa broke up the coalition. Soon after he reconciled his differences with Jawara and the PPP, and in 1963 was appointed Gambia Commissioner to the United Kingdom. After returning to the Gambia in 1964, he retired from active politics and devoted his energies to the church.

FINDEN, HARRY. A very successful trader and merchant in Bathurst during the third quarter of the 19th century. Barely literate, he was, nevertheless, elected leader of the Igbo Friendly Society in 1849 in succession to Thomas Reffell. He was one of the most important Gambians in the protest movement of the 1870s against Britain's proposed exchange of the Gambia for French territory. In concert with Joseph Reffell, Thomas Brown, and J. D. Richards, he helped design and sign the many memorials to the British government officials in Bathurst and London stating the opposition of the Bathurst trading community to any such exchange.

FITZGERALD, CHARLES. Secretary of the Gambia Committee which opposed the cession of the Gambia to France in 1875-76. He was a retired officer of the West Indies Regiment who in 1875 authored a widely circulated pamphlet entitled, The Gambia and Its Proposed Cession to France. It is probable that he had written an earlier pamphlet issued anonymously in 1870 entitled, Has the Crown the Right to Cede the Gambia to France?

FIVE-FRANC PIECE. A very handsome French coin which was accepted by an Order-in-Council as legal tender in the Gambia. The exchange rate was set at three shillings, ten and one-half pence. By the opening of the 20th century, it comprised over 80 percent of the total money in circulation in the Gambia. By the end of World War I, the franc had fallen in value, but nothing was done in the Gambia to make the official rate conform to the world rate. Issuance of the new West African alloyed coins in 1920 did not drive out the older currency. The Gambia was the only place in the world where the five-franc piece could be exchanged at a rate approximately 1-3/4 times its real value, and the area was thus flooded by the coins. They ceased to be valid for overseas transfers in March 1921, and in April their importation was prohibited. These actions did not halt the influx of the coins. Eventually in 1922, the British decided to demonetize, and called in all the five-franc pieces at the legal rate. The cost of the failure of British authorities to act promptly had to be borne by the Gambia. The demonetization cost the Gambia over Ł200,000 at a time when social and economic improvements were being denied ostensibly because of a lack of funds.

FODI KABBA   see   DUMBUYA, FODI KABBA

FODI SILLA   see   TOURE, FODI SILLA

FONI. One of the nine Mandingo kingdoms along the south bank of the Gambia River in the early 19th century, lying south of Bintang Bolon and adjoining Kombo in the west. During the latter stages of the Soninke-Marabout Wars, the traditional rulers were overthrown and most of the territory was controlled by adherents of either Fodi Kabba or Fodi Silla. However, the large Jola population resident there resisted conversion and was never completely conquered. In 1887, most of the Jola chiefs placed themselves under British protection and seven years later after Fodi Silla's defeat, they refused sanctuary to his forces, forcing him to flee to the Casamance. The non-Jola leaders also assumed a pro-British position in the 1890s, thus depriving Fodi Kabba of much needed support. In the 20th-century British reorganization of the Protectorate, Foni was divided into six districts--Foni Brefet, Foni Bintang, Foni Karani, Foni Kansala, Foni Bondali, and Foni Jarrol--each under the direction of a chief.

FOON, KEBBA WALLY. A Bathurst accountant and Wolof political leader, born in 1922 and educated at the Boys High School in Bathurst. He worked as a junior clerk in the Treasury Department and on the Gambian steamers of the travelling Post Office. Early in World War II he joined the merchant marine and in 1945 received an appointment to Posts and Telecommunications in London. From 1948 to

1952 he served as clerk-accountant in the British Ministry
of Agriculture. Becoming a certified accountant, he
joined a firm of London chartered accountants, and in
1954 returned to the Gambia to establish their office in
Bathurst. In 1955 he started his own firm. In Britain
he had formed the Gambia League and worked closely with
nationalists of other territories against continued British
control of African states. In 1956, he and other educated
Gambians formed the National Party which, however, ceased
to be a factor in politics by 1960. In the latter 1950s, he
and his wife, Marion, published a small, informative Bathurst newspaper. In the elections of 1962 and 1966, Foon
associated himself with the United Party of P. S. N'Jie,
but was defeated in his attempt to gain a seat in the
House. With the failure of the United Party, he withdrew
from active politics to pursue his business career.

FORDE, DR. ROBERT M. Surgeon and medical researcher
who had previously served in the Gold Coast from 1891
to 1895. He was appointed to be Colonial Surgeon in the
Gambia in 1895 and became Senior Medical Officer in 1904.
In April 1901, he discovered in the blood of a European
patient a trypanosome, carried by the tsetse fly, that was
the cause of "sleeping sickness." Forde's discovery of
the Trypanosome gambiense was the first major break-
through in the treatment of this deadly disease whose
cause had previously been a mystery.

FORO. The title given to a caste in Mandingo society. They
are freeborn members of a lineage comparable to the Wolof
badolo.

FORSTER, SAMUEL JOHN. Lawyer born in Bathurst in 1912
and educated at the Methodist Boys High School, Fourah
Bay College, and the Middle Temple in London. He was a
Colonial Magistrate in the Gambia from 1947-53 and was
the Liaison Officer in charge of the Gambia Office in London from 1959-62. Forster moved to Sierra Leone in 1963
when he was appointed a Police Magistrate, a position he
held until created a Pusine Judge in 1966. He continued
to reside in Freetown and pursue his judicial career outside the Gambia until 1982 when he was one of the judges
chosen to hear the cases of those accused in the coup
attempt.

FORSTER, SMITH AND COMPANY. One of the oldest British trading firms in the Gambia, it was operative from the early 1820s. After the death of Matthew Forster, the senior partner, the firm's business was drastically reduced and its assets transferred in 1870 to another British firm of Lintott, Spink and Company.

FOWLIS, ROSAMOND AROENKEH. Teacher and union organizer, born in Bathurst in 1910, educated Dobson St. Day School, Methodist Girls High School, Leicester Domestic Science College, U.K., teacher of Domestic Science 1931-65; organizer of nutrition classes and domestic science for women and girls in rural areas, compiler of booklet on nutrition; President of Gambia Teachers Union, 1941-44. Member Gambia Education Board, 1945; Member Board of Governors Gambia High School, 1967-68; awarded MBE, 1953.

FULADU. Late 19th-century state created by Alfa Molloh with the support of al Hajj Umar Tall, the leader of the Tijaniyya movement within West African Islam and head of the Tucolor Empire and the rulers of the Futa Jallon to whom Fuladu remained tributary until 1893. By 1872 Alfa had conquered three small Mandinka states on the south bank of the Gambia River--Tomani, Kantora, and Jimara. These conquests largely accomplished by his son Musa laid the foundation for the kingdom. Musa defended and even extended the boundaries of the kingdom during the mid-phase of the Soninke-Marabout Wars. The death of Alfa in 1891 brought civil war to Fuladu since Musa refused to accept the overlordship of his uncle Bakari, who had inherited the throne. Withdrawing southward to a fortified town, Hamdallai in Casamance, Musa continually raided into Fuladu and after more than a decade of fighting killed Bakari and other members of the family and proclaimed himself king in 1892. The following year he ended the tribute paid to the rulers of the Futa Jallon. Musa then created a centralized, autocratic state noted not only for its efficiency, but also for the ruthlessness of the king's rule.

    After the partition of Senegambia in 1889, Musa chose to maintain good relations with both European powers, especially the French, even participating in the punitive expedition against his old enemy, Fodi Kabba. Eventually this cooperation did not keep the French from sending forces into the interior to build a military post at Hamdallai. Musa left the Casamance and retreated into the Gambia, where the British recognized him as the ruler of a much smaller state of Fuladu. Under British control he continued his autocracy until the reports of his actions against his subjects caused them to remove him and he was sent into exile in Sierra Leone. Ultimately, the small kingdom was divided by the British into three parts and administered by three chiefs responsible to the District Commissioners of MacCarthy and Upper River Divisions.

FULBE (Fulani, Peul, Fula). A pastoral people whose homeland was in the vicinity of the upper Senegal River and who speak a variant of the Niger-Kordofanian language family. They were the dominant group in the ancient kingdom of Tekrur. After the overthrow of Tekrur, the Fulbe created a series of smaller states from the western segment of that state where they continued in power until the Tucolor majority in those areas seized power and established a strict Muslim rule in the Futa Toro. Between the 13th and 18th centuries, large numbers of Fulbe in a series of long, complicated migrations, established themselves throughout the western and central Sudan as far eastward as the Cameroons. They were an important element in the population of Macina, were the base population for the theocracies of the Futa Jallon, and were present in large numbers in the Hausa states of northern Nigeria. Usuman dan Fodio, himself a Fulbe in Gobir, used them in the early 19th century as the cadre of his jihad which overran the Hausa states and created an empire in northern Nigeria. The Fulbe were present in large numbers in the upper Gambia region in the 19th century where, although living in Mandingo states, they maintained close ties with both the Futa Toro and Futa Jallon. Alfa Molloh in his revolt of the 1860s used the Fulbe to create his kingdom of Fuladu.

FULBE BURURE. A dialect group of the Fulbe who in the latter 19th century migrated through Fuladu in great numbers and were the principal owners of cattle in the area in the 1870s. They participated in the Fulbe revolt against the Mandingo, but refused to serve Alfa Molloh whose antecedents they held to be less pure than their own. Many of the Burure left Fuladu in the 1880s after their leaders quarrelled with Alfa Molloh.

FULBE FIRDU. A dialect group of the Fulbe which today
    number over 30,000 in the upper Gambia River area. In
    the late 18th and early 19th centuries, they had migrated
    in great numbers into the old Mandingo kingdoms of To-
    mani and Jimara. They were semi-sedentary, normally
    spending 15 or more years in one location, and they tend-
    ed to intermarry with other peoples in that locale. The
    Fulbe Firdu comprised the main support group for Alfa
    Molloh's rebellion against his Mandingo overlords.

FULBE FUTO. A dialect group of the Fulbe originally from
    the Futa Jallon region. In the latter 19th century they
    settled in the southern section of Fuladu in what is now
    the Casamance. Before the Fulbe uprising of the 1860s,
    groups of the Fulbe Futo continually raided into the
    riverine areas. Others of this group had temporarily
    settled near the river to plant peanuts. In the early
    years of his ascendency, Alfa Molloh paid tribute to the
    head of the Fulbe Futo in the Futa Jallon.

FUTA JALLON. A highland area in what is now Guinea with
    elevations up to 5000 feet. It is also the source of the
    Gambia, Senegal, and Niger Rivers. In the early 18th
    century, Fulbe reformers created there a theocracy with
    the state controlled by elected almamis. The Futa Jallon
    experience acted as a model for Islamic reformers in the
    Futa Toro, northern Nigeria, and the Gambia. Many Fulbe
    from the Futa Jallon regularly migrated to the area which
    would later become southern Fuladu. These Fulbe Futo
    became an important factor in the success of Alfa Molloh,
    and the Almamy of Futa Jallon loaned him fighting men to
    oppose the Mandingo traditional rulers. The state of Futa
    Jallon remained independent until the Almamy placed it
    under French protection in 1888.

FUTA TORO. An area adjacent to the middle Senegal River
    inhabited largely by Tucolor and Fulbe people. In 1776,
    a new theocratic state was created in the Futa Toro led
    by Marabouts of the Qadiriyya tariq. Later in the 19th
    century it became the centrum of the empire established
    by the Tijaniyya leader Al Hajj Umar Tall. The Futa Toro
    acted as a training ground for most of the Marabouts who
    wanted to convert the "pagan" peoples of the Senegambia
    region. In addition, the rulers of Futa Toro gave direct
    military assistance to some of the war chiefs of the Gam-
    bia during the Soninke-Marabout Wars.

-G-

GNP   see   GAMBIA NATIONAL PARTY

GNU   see   GAMBIA NATIONAL UNION

GPMB   see   GAMBIA PRODUCE MARKETING BOARD

GPP   see   GAMBIA PEOPLES PARTY

GWU   see   GAMBIA WORKERS' UNION

GAMBIA ADVENTURERS. A joint stock company which was
   allowed by the Royal Adventurers in 1668 to assume the
   monopoly of trade in the areas adjacent to the Gambia
   River. In 1684 after little profit and much litigation in
   London, the Gambia Adventurers and their parent company
   relinquished their trading monopoly to the Royal African
   Company.

GAMBIA LABOUR UNION. A Bathurst-based general union
   organized by Edward Small in 1929. In that year the
   union called the first strike in Gambian history and Small
   was successful in negotiating higher salaries for artisans
   and river craft workers. Despite this minor initial success the union was a very weak vehicle for protest during its entire existence. This was due to world economic
   conditions and the generally hostile attitude of the British
   authorities. The economic extension of Small's political
   activity and his position in the union helped him to be
   selected to the general executive council of the International Confederation of Free Trade Unions in 1932.

GAMBIA MINERALS COMPANY. British company formed to
   explore and exploit the ilmenite deposits near Brufut in
   1954. Ilmenite ore, the source of rutile and titanium
   oxide, was in short supply, and the major producers in
   India had raised prices on the ore. Gambian deposits
   were found to be marginal, but construction began, nevertheless, in 1956 on a railroad, electric dry mill, and
   other facilities. Although the company invested over one
   million pounds, the entire operation was closed down in
   1959 ostensibly because the world price of rutile had fallen to the point where it was unprofitable to continue
   operation.

GAMBIA NATIONAL PARTY (GNP).   A Colony oriented party
   formed by a small number of educated Bathurst citizens
   in 1956.   It was most effective in the various deliberations
   which led to the revision of the Constitution prior to the
   1960 elections.   The party never had a popular base of
   support and broke apart because of internal dissentions
   on the eve of the 1960 elections.

GAMBIA NATIONAL UNION (GNU).   A small Colony based
   political party formed in 1961 to present alternatives to
   both the United Party and the People's Progressive Party.
   However, in the elections of 1962 and for some time afterward, it cooperated with the United Party.   The Gambia
   National Union was never large, and by 1965, most of its
   members had either joined the United Party or had ceased
   to be active.   By 1967, with the retirement of some key
   leaders, the party had ceased to function.

GAMBIA PEOPLES PARTY (GPP).   A political organization
   formed in early 1986 to prepare for the general elections
   to be held in May 1987.   The leaders were Howsoon
   Semega-Janneh, Lamin Saho, and Hassan Musa Camara,
   all former PPP members and previous members of the
   central government.   Camara, who had been a member of
   the PPP Central Committee and Vice-President for seven
   years, was chosen to head the new party.

GAMBIA PRODUCE MARKETING BOARD (GPMB).   Previously
   called the Gambia Oilseeds Marketing Board, it was created by the British colonial regime in 1949 to act as the
   chief purchasing agent for the peanut crop.   The appointive board establishes a fixed payment per unit of de-
   corticated and undecorticated nuts and all peanut by-
   products based upon the previous year's experience.
   GPMB has always followed the practice of paying immediately the bulk of the purchase price to the farmers.
   Senegal, by contrast, for many years paid higher prices,
   but on a three-payment system.   A large portion of the
   Sine and Saloum crop was brought to the Gambia for the
   immediate payment.   The name of the board was changed
   in 1971 when it became necessary for the government to
   fund and purchase the ever increasing Gambian rice crop
   as well as the peanut crop.

GAMBIA REGIMENT.   In 1901, the British recruited and

trained a unit of company strength which formed a part
of the Sierra Leone Battalion of the Royal West African
Frontier Force. During World War I, the Gambia Company
saw active service in Cameroon and East Africa. In 1939,
the company was stationed in Sierra Leone, but in the following year was posted to Bathurst where it served as the
cadre for the First Battalion of the Gambia Regiment. In
1941, the Second Battalion was formed. The First Battalion in 1943 was attached to the Sixth Brigade of the 81st
(West Africa) Division in Nigeria. From there, the division was moved to the Far East, and the Battalion took
part in the eight day defense of Frontier Hill in Burma.
The Second Battalion was also sent to the Far East and
attached to the 81st Division. It took part in the victory
at Myohaung and in the liberation of Rangoon. Both units
returned to the Gambia in 1945, and after demobilization,
select elements were combined to form once again the Gambia Company of the Sierra Leone Battalion. In 1950, "A"
Company became a separate entity and was presented with
its colors in April 1951, the only unit of company strength
to have them. The Company was broken up for financial
reasons on the recommendation of Governor Wyn Harris,
and a portion of the soldiers were regrouped in 1958 as
the Field Force, a specialized unit of the police force.

GAMBIA WORKERS UNION (GWU). The key labor organization in the Gambia. It was formed in 1957 by M. E. Jallow and some associates, and within a short period had
become an effective representative for many of the workers in Bathurst and at the peanut shipping ports of Kaur
and Kuntaur. In 1961, the British authorities charged
that Jallow in the course of a strike of dock workers had
incited them to violence. Although found guilty, he was
given only a nominal fine, and his union was successful in
gaining many of its demand from the government. The
Gambia Workers Union stood aloof from direct participation
in the elections of 1960 and 1962, but it appeared that by
1964 Jallow was prepared to use the union in a more open
political manner. However, he accepted the position of
Secretary General with the African Regional Office of the
International Confederation of Free Trade Unions in that
year. Without him the union withdrew from overt political
activity in the latter 1960s, and its leaders became concerned only with the problems of labor.

GARBA-JAHUMPA, IBRIMAH MOMODOU. Teacher, labor
   leader, and politician, born in Bathurst in 1912 of a family which had migrated from Senegal in 1816. He attended
   Koranic school, primary, and secondary schools in Bathurst,
   and completed work at the Teachers Training College in
   1936. He became a teacher and taught until 1949 in
   Bathurst and Georgetown except for a brief period during
   World War II when he was associated with BOAC. He was
   Secretary of the Gambia Labor Union from 1939 to 1945
   and was a member of the International Confederation of
   Free Trade Unions. Garba-Jahumpa's political activities
   began in 1935 when he became Assistant Secretary of the
   Bathurst Rate Payers Association. He was appointed a
   member of the Bathurst Town Council in 1942, was elected
   a member in 1947, and in 1959 became the first Chairman
   of the Council. He won one of the two elected seats to
   the Legislative Council in the elections of 1951, and three
   months after the election was instrumental in coalescing a
   number of Muslim organizations into the Muslim Congress
   Party. Garba-Jahumpa was reelected in 1954 and was appointed Minister of Agriculture and Natural Resources, a
   post he held until the elections of 1960. Two months before that election, the Muslim Congress merged with the
   Democratic Party to form the Democratic Congress Alliance.
   However, this coalition was not successful since it elected
   only one member from the Colony area.
      In 1961, an agreement was reached with the People's
   Progressive Party whereby in future elections, no PPP
   candidate would stand against a DCA-sponsored candidate.
   Despite this, the DCA in 1962 returned only one member
   to the House of Assembly, and Garba-Jahumpa was defeated by a United Party candidate. Soon afterward,
   Garba-Jahumpa broke with the DCA and organized the
   Congress Party. With this as a vehicle, Garba-Jahumpa
   was elected to the House of Assembly in 1964. By 1968,
   he had resolved his differences with the PPP through
   compromise. The Congress Party was disbanded and
   Garba-Jahumpa became Minister of Health and Social Welfare. In early 1973, he was appointed Minister of Finance,
   a position he held for almost five years. After being replaced by Momadau Cham, he retired from active politics.

GARRISON SCHOOL. The school created by the British for
   the education and training of African soldiers stationed

in the Gambia. The school at Bathurst was particularly important during Governor D'Arcy's tenure in producing a small number of competent African noncommissioned officers.

GEREGIA. The site of a Portuguese settlement on the south bank of the Bintang Bolon approximately twenty miles from the village of Bintang. It is conjectured that the present-day village of Kansala is near the site of Geregia. In the 1650s the area near Geregia was a favorite trading locale for the English. They established a factory there as early as 1689 and continued to maintain trading posts there throughout the early 18th century.

GEWEL. A Wolof term for persons whose responsibilities included everything to do with communications. They preserved the local history, genealogies, and social rankings and were those through whom was passed the stories of previous generations. They were also the musicians in charge of the war dancing and royal drums. Called griots by the French, they were attached to particular noble families, receiving protection and generous pay for their many services. Despite this, until the colonial period they were one section of a low-born caste called nenyo. Thus, they were required to live in a particular part of a village, could not marry outside their caste, and were denied the usual forms of burial after death.

GOLBERY, S. M. X. An official of the French trading company in the Senegambia during the mid-1780s. In 1802 he published a two-volume account of his experiences entitled, Fragments d'un voyage en Afrique.

GOMES, DIEGO. A one-time page to Prince Henry of Portugal, he led an expedition which entered the Gambia estuary in 1457. Gomes met with chiefs who the year before had received Cadamosto, travelled upriver to Kantora, and traded for considerable gold. His reports of the rich gold fields of the interior combined with the gold he brought back helped convince Europe of the wealth to be had in interior trade. Gomes' reports also led to the first two Portuguese missionaries being sent to the Gambia in an abortive attempt to convert the riverine Africans.

GOULDSBURY, VALESIUS S. (Surgeon-Major). Administrator

of the Gambia from 1877 until 1884. In 1880, the Governor in Chief, Sir Samuel Rowe, proposed that part of the
Ł19,000 surplus in the Gambian treasury be used to finance an expedition into the hinterland as far as the Futa
Jallon with the purpose of investigating trading possibili-
ties and entering into friendly relations with African rulers. When this was approved, Administrator Gouldsbury
was chosen to lead the exploration. In 1881, Gouldsbury
followed the path laid down by his instructions and proceeded as far as the Futa Jallon. He made a number of
treaties with the rulers of the upper river and the Futa
Jallon. The expedition was valuable only because it gave
the government up-to-date information on the events then
transpiring in the interior and because it confirmed what
Lieutenant-Governor MacDonnell had said in 1849 about
the paucity of trading opportunities there. Gouldsbury
believed that any profits to be made there would be more
than offset by the expense involved. His negative report
helped support the general British attitude that the interior lands were worthless and predisposed the Colonial
Office to adopt a quiescent attitude toward French expansion into the interior during the 1880s.

GRANT, ALEXANDER (Captain; later Lieutenant Colonel).
Captain Grant was sent from Goree in March 1816 with
two officers, 50 men of the African Corps, and 24 artisans with orders to reoccupy Fort James, in order to
protect British trade rights to the Gambia and to check
the trade in slaves. Grant arranged with the ruler of
Barra for the reoccupation by agreeing to pay approximately Ł75 per year. He soon discovered that the fort
was almost beyond repair and suggested to his superiors
that Banjul be occupied instead. Colonel Brereton with
30 more men joined Grant in April and together they negotiated with the king of Kombo the cession of the island
for a payment of approximately Ł25 per year. On April
23, 1816, Grant took formal possession of the island and
began work on barracks and gun emplacements. The king
of Barra allowed the British to take stone from Dog Island for their construction work. The British at Goree
advertised special privileges for merchants who established themselves at the new settlement called Bathurst.
By early 1819, there were 700 civilians in the town and
within a decade, over 1800. Grant was responsible for
laying out the basic pattern of the city of Bathurst with

its streets named after Waterloo generals. He built the earliest section of Government House, and the barracks he constructed were long used as government offices. Grant took the lead role in urging merchants towards legitimate trade, and from the beginning used all the forces at his command to stop the riverine slave trade. He also encouraged the missionary activities of the Society of Friends and the Wesleyans. In 1823, he negotiated the occupation of the island of Lemaine (renamed MacCarthy) and ordered the construction of a mud fort, called Fort George, which was then manned by a dozen soldiers. Grant also served as Acting Governor of Sierra Leone in 1820 and again in 1821. He was promoted to Major in the second West India Regiment just before he turned over command of the Gambia garrison to Captain Findley in 1823.

GRAY, SIR JOHN M. A Justice in the High Court of the Gambia in the 1930s. He is most remembered for his long, detailed, scholarly work, A History of the Gambia, published in 1940. It has remained the standard work on Gambian history through the 19th century.

GRIOT   see   GEWEL

GRIS-GRIS. Charms which the wearer believes have the power to either ward off a specific evil or to enable him to perform certain tasks. These were originally in traditional society compounded by someone who was believed to have unique powers in communicating with the spirit world. Today many Muslims wear small leather-bound verses of the Koran which they have received from a Marabout.

GROUNDNUTS. A spreading, hairy, annual leguminous herb (Archis hypogasa) which provides the main cash crop of Gambian farmers. The plant is native to Brazil and was brought to Europe in the 16th century from where it was taken to all parts of the world. The groundnut, or peanut, was introduced to the Gambia by the Portuguese and was noted by such early English visitors as Jobson and Moore. However, its cultivation as a cash crop did not begin until the great increase in demand for fats and oils which occurred in Europe in the last 75 years of the 19th century. The first shipment of peanuts from the Gambia was in 1830, worth only slightly more than £10. By 1890,

over 18,000 tons worth Ł130,000 were exported. In the
1960s, the annual crop of the Gambia was over 100,000
tons. Peanuts are planted in April or May just before
the rainy season. The Mandinka and Jola plant the peanuts in ridges while the Wolof plant them on the flat.
Weeding is a continuous process during the growing season. Harvesting is normally done by digging the plants
by hand, generally during October. The plants are then
stacked to dry, and threshing is done after the trading
season opens in December. The nuts are then sacked and
transported to the buying stations.

GUELOWAR. The title of the matrilineage from which the
    rulers of Sine and Saloum were chosen. This matrilineage
    was historically that which had led a northward moving
    Mandingo migration which in the 13th or 14th centuries
    encountered the southward migrating Serer. It is from
    this meeting that the complex political institutions of the
    Serer states can be dated.

GUINEA COMPANY (British). Formed in 1651 by the Com-
    monwealth in expectation of riches to be gained from West
    African trade. Two trading expeditions were sent to
    Gambia, a factory established on Bintang Bolon, and
    traders sent as far into the interior as Barrakunda. A
    series of accidents destroyed much of the trade goods,
    large numbers of the Europeans were incapacitated by ill-
    ness and many died, and finally in early 1652, Prince Ru-
    pert and a small royalist fleet entered the Gambia River
    and seized the company ships. Following this disaster,
    the Commonwealth abandoned all attempts to trade in the
    Gambia.

GUM TRADE. Established in the 16th century, the trade in
    gum arabic (derived from the Acacia arabica tree) had by
    the 18th century become very important for some West Af-
    rican traders. The Royal African Company began to trade
    for this item at the station of Portendic in Mauritania.
    Both French and British gum merchants suffered because
    of the European wars of the 18th century. One of Gover-
    nor Faidherbe's first goals in the 1850s was to end the
    exclusive power of the Mauritanian sheikhs over this trade.
    Soon afterward in 1857, Britain relinquished its rights to
    the trade at Portendic in return for French abandonment
    of their station of Albreda on the Gambia River.

GUNJUR. A town in southern Kombo which was the main
   base of operations of the young Marabout Fodi Kabba in
   the 1850s who in collaboration with Omar of Sabaji almost
   defeated the British forces in Bathurst. It continued to
   be a Marabout stronghold during the 1860s and was a
   particularly important base during the final conquest of
   the Soninkes in Kombo during the 1870s. Fodi Silla had
   by this time come to control Gunjur and his activities
   against the Boundary Commission finally brought a British
   punitive expedition into Kombo. Gunjur and Fodi Silla's
   other main towns were taken in 1894, and he was forced
   to flee to the Casamance where he was captured by the
   French.

                              -H-

HAJJ. The pilgrimage to Mecca, one of the five obligatory
   requirements of Islam. Senegambians were among the
   first West Africans to travel to Mecca, some as early as
   the 11th century. Four major routes across the Sahara
   were used by the pilgrims on this long, dangerous journey, each converging on Cairo. Today, charter air
   flights are available to the faithful from the Senegambia.
   Where only a few years ago the journey was still long and
   hazardous, the hajj now is relatively safe and inexpensive.
   Although a few believers still stay in Mecca to study,
   most are satisfied to join with fellow worshipers from all
   over the world in a one- to three-week excursion. Those
   who have made the pilgrimage are referred to by the
   title al Hajj (male) or al Hajja (female). In a few cases
   this title has been incorporated as a part of a given name
   and does not indicate that the person has been to Mecca.

HALF DIE. A portion of Banjul (Bathurst) adjacent to Jolof
   Town at the lower end of Wellington Street and bordered
   on one side by the Atlantic Ocean and on another by the
   Gambia River. This area, also called Moka Town, was
   inhabited by the poorer residents of the city. Until pro-
   tective measures were taken in the 20th century, Half Die
   was nothing but a sandbank in the dry season and a
   swamp during the rains. Ostensibly the section received
   its name because of the high mortality rate there in the
   19th century.

HANNO. Carthaginian soldier and mariner who in about
500 B.C. was commissioned to investigate the western
coastline of Africa. According to writing on a stone
column at the Temple of Baal in Carthage, Hanno's ships
reached the Chertes (Senegal) River and then the Bam-
botus, "a large and broad river" full of crocodiles and
hippopotami. This latter river was probably the Gambia.
H. Richmond Palmer, in The Carthaginian Voyage to West
Africa, comments that Hanno probably reached the vicinity
of Sierra Leone before turning back.

HAVELOCK, SIR ARTHUR E. Governor of the West African
Settlements (Sierra Leone and the Gambia) from 1881 to
1884. He was a delegate to the 1881 Commission to deal
with the French over the Sierra Leone boundary. The
question of a generalized exchange of territory including
the Gambia by both powers was discussed, but the British
refused to consider ceding the Gambia at that time.

HELM, HENRY (HEINRICH). A Prussian born and natural-
ized British citizen and resident of Bathurst who was responsible after 1870 for managing the Gambian affairs of
Thomas Chown and Sons. He became a member of the
Legislative Council in 1878 and continued the Chowns'
opposition to any cession of the Gambia to France.

HEMMING, AUGUSTUS. A senior British civil servant in the
Colonial Office and an expert on West African affairs. He
was one of the two British delegates to the Paris Conference which produced the Convention of 1889 that drew
the boundaries of the Gambia.

HODGES, SAMUEL. A soldier in the 4th West India Regiment
stationed in the Gambia in 1866 to support Colonel D'Arcy's
attack upon Amer Faal's stronghold of Tubab Kolon. On
July 26, artillery fire having proved to have little effect
on the stockade, D'Arcy called for volunteers to advance
under fire and chop a hole in the wooden walls with axes.
Hodges was one of the 17 men who volunteered. Only he
and another soldier named Boswell reached the wall, and
they began to hew away while the defenders concentrated
a heavy fire on them. Boswell was killed, but Hodges
continued his work and made a hole in the wall. D'Arcy
then led his men through the gap, following Hodges who

also breached two of the inner walls with his axe. For
this display of conspicious bravery, Hodges was awarded
the Victoria Cross.

HOLMES, MAJOR ROBERT. Appointed in 1661 as commander
of a small fleet of ships outfitted by the Royal Adventurers of England Trading into Africa to establish their dominance on the Gambia River. He occupied Dog Island,
cultivated the friendship of the ruler of Kombo, and finally forced the surrender of the Courlanders on St. Andrew's Island. Holmes renamed the island after James,
the Duke of York. Although Holmes' action against the
Courlanders was unauthorized, English possession of the
Courlander's fort and trading stations was used to force
the cession of the Courlander rights to the English in 1664.
In 1663, Holmes was again sent with two ships to the Gambia to unload stores and ascertain the situation of the garrison he had left. Upon being informed of the presence
of a hostile Dutch ship in Gambian waters, Holmes took
his three ships northward and captured the Dutch trading
entrepôt of Goree. His actions had a precipitating effect
on the second English-Dutch conflict, for the States General dispatched Admiral de Ruyter and 13 ships to recap-
ture Goree. Although de Ruyter by-passed James Island,
this victory was one of the first in the second trade war
between the two great maritime powers.

HORTON, DR. JAMES AFRICANUS. Medical officer, writer,
and businessman, born in Gloucester, Sierra Leone in
1835. He attended village schools, the Church Missionary
Grammar School, and Fourah Bay College. He was one of
three Africans selected by the British in 1855 for medical
training. In 1858 he completed work at Kings College,
London, and was admitted to the Royal College of Surgeons. He later completed his doctorate at Edinburgh in
1859 and entered the army as a staff assistant-surgeon
the same year and was posted to the Gold Coast. He took
part in the Ashanti War of 1864 and was sent to the Gambia the following year. He accompanied the British troops
sent to MacCarthy Island to counter the threats to British
hegemony there. After the soldiers were withdrawn, Horton stayed behind as commandant, entered into friendly
relations with neighboring chiefs, and helped organize a
provisional government for the island. When the regular
British magistrate arrived in June 1866, Horton left and

arrived in Bathurst in time to give his professional aid
during the yellow fever epidemic. In 1867, he returned
to the Gold Coast. Until his death in 1883, he continued
to be a spokesman for the Africans.

HOUGHTON, MAJOR DONALD. A British army officer and
explorer. He was stationed at Goree in 1780 when ordered to Bintang with 80 men and four small ships to cut
timber. While there he was forced by a French man-of-
war to sink his ships and take refuge with the Jola.
Aided by them, Houghton managed to drive off the French
landing parties and was later rescued by a British warship. In 1790, Houghton was chosen by the Association
for Promoting the Discovery of the Interior Parts of Africa to try to open communications between the Gambia and
Timbuktu. He travelled to Medina near Barrakunda Falls
and from there proceeded to Bambuk where he either died
of disease or was murdered.

HUNGRY SEASON. Concentration on groundnuts (peanuts),
the one cash crop of the Gambia, poor roads, and a faulty
system of distribution of local surpluses of foods led to
chronic food shortages by the early 1930s for a portion of
the year just before harvest time. In some of the upper
river areas near famine conditions prevailed during this
"hungry season." To offset this, the Colonial government
had to import large quantities of rice, usually of an in-
ferior quality, which was distributed to the people. Beginning in the 1950s, more farmers were induced to plant
rice, fertilizers were used, ox-plowing schools were started, and foreign rice experts were brought to the Protectorate. This concentration on rice production, coupled
with more improved market facilities and all-weather roads,
has ended the hungry season which was once such an accepted part of the lives of so many Gambians.

HUNTLEY, SIR HENRY VERE. Lieutenant-Governor of the
Gambia in 1840, succeeding William Mackie who had governed for only six months. Huntley found the Colony in
debt, the problems of the liberated Africans still unsolved,
and British prestige in the upper river at a very low level.
Huntley provided space for the resettlement of liberated
Africans by convincing Suling Jata, the ruler of Kombo,
to cede to the Crown the district now known as Kombo St.
Mary. In the MacCarthy Island area there was a brief

period of violence between various factions during which the chief of Nyanibantang was killed. After Huntley ordered the British there to maintain strict neutrality between feuding factions and denied the island as a place of sanctuary, British prestige was soon restored. He reinforced the garrison at MacCarthy Island, gained the cession of land for a small fort at Kataba, and entered into a treaty of protection with the chief. This latter treaty, however, was disavowed by the Colonial Office. In 1842, Huntley was transferred to Prince Edward Island.

HUTTON, WILLIAM. Administrator temporarily in charge of the British administration at Bathurst in 1829. Without consulting the Colonial Office, he had induced Bathurst merchants to subscribe some Ł7,000 of goods for interior trade, contingent upon satisfactory treaties with hinterland chiefs. In April and May of 1829, he entered into agreements which would allow the British to build factories at Kantalikunda, and the king of Wuli ceded Fattatenda outright. Hutton's agreements were repudiated by the British government and he was later dismissed from the service because of questions over his handling of public finance.

-I-

IBRAHIMA, ALFA. One of the powerful Fulbe rulers of the Futa Jallon in the late 19th century who played an important role in the success of Alfa Molloh in his wars against the traditional Mandingo rulers of Jimara, Tomani, and Eropina. In the late 1860s, he sent his son with Fulbe reinforcements to aid Alfa Molloh's armies, and continued to support the Fulbe throughout the 1870s. In 1879, large numbers of Ibrahima's troops took part in the campaign against Simotto Moro at Tubakuta. Although Alfa Molloh did not consider himself subject to Ibrahima, there was a positive client relationship between Fuladu and the Futa Jallon.

ILER. The name of a tool with a short handle and an inverted, heart-shaped blade used in cultivation by Wolof and Mandingo peanut farmers in Saloum and the Gambia. The iler is the main tool used to clear weeds and also to loosen the soil around the plants at harvest time.

ILMENITE. A mineral which is the source of rutile, titanium
    oxide, and zircon. It is found in marginal quantities in
    the Gambia. Between 1956 and 1959, the Gambia Minerals
    Company operated a mine and plant near Brufut for pro-
    cessing ilmenite. Mining operations ceased because of a
    fall in the world market price of rutile and zircon.

INDIRECT RULE. The term which describes the general ad-
    ministrative policy followed by Great Britain in governing
    the bulk of its African territories. In theory, African
    traditional rulers, with the supervision of European Dis-
    trict Officers, would be authorized to continue to make
    the basic administrative and legal decisions for their peo-
    ple. In the Gambia this was complicated because the
    Soninke-Marabout Wars had disturbed and in some cases
    destroyed the older kingdoms and their ruling classes.
    The first attempt at Indirect Rule came with the appoint-
    ment of Travelling Commissioners in 1893 and the Protec-
    torate Ordinance of 1894. Subsequent Ordinances had
    created by 1945 a system whereby the bulk of the Gambia
    was governed by 35 appointed chiefs. Legislation spon-
    sored by Governors Palmer and Richards from 1933 to 1935
    brought the theory and practice of government in line with
    the concepts of Lugard and Sir Donald Cameron. A Senior
    Commissioner to provide continuity of policy and centrali-
    zation of planning was appointed in 1944. In the same
    year the government established the annual Conference of
    Protectorate Chiefs.

ISMAIL, AL HAJJ. A Mauritanian teacher who in the early
    1850s travelled through the western Sudan preaching a
    jihad against the infidel. He probably never visited the
    Gambia, but one of his agents, Omar, took up residence
    in Sabaji where he, in conjunction with the Marabouts of
    Gunjur, planned the attack in 1855 upon the Soninkes of
    Kombo which almost succeeded in taking Bathurst. Short-
    ly afterward, Ismail was captured by the French and sent
    into exile to Cayenne.

                              -J-

JACK, ALIEU SULAYMAN. Civil servant and politician,
    born at Bathurst in 1922 into a Muslim Wolof family. He
    was educated at the Roman Catholic mission school and

joined the Civil Service during World War II. In 1950, he began his political career when elected to the Bathurst Town Council. He early associated himself with the People's Progressive Party and became the Speaker of the House of Assembly after the elections of 1962. In the government reorganization following the Republic plebiscite, he was named Minister for Works and Communications.

JALLOW, MOMADOU EBRIMA. A Gambian labor leader, born in Georgetown in June 1928 and educated through the secondary level at St. Augustine's School. He joined the Civil Service as a clerk in the Education Department and later in the Income Tax Division. He also worked in the mid-1950s as a secretary-accountant for private firms in Bathurst. At the urging of friends, he formed the Gambia Construction Employees Society which led to the creation in late 1957 of the Gambia Workers Union. Although with little experience of unionism, Jallow was able in 1958 to negotiate a number of favorable contracts with employers. In late 1958 he attended a four-month course in trade unionism at Kampala and began to make contacts outside the Gambia. Throughout 1959 he concentrated on building union strength among the dock workers and daily paid employees. The following year, at the height of the peanut season, his union conducted the first successful large-scale strike in the Gambia. This strike gained a substantial increase in the wages of daily workers and eventually led to the formation of Joint Industrial Councils for the arbitration of labor disputes. The British government decision to indict him for taking part in a riot merely increased his popularity among Gambians. Jallow's decision not to enter politics at this period in Gambian history was crucial since his popularity might have created a political vehicle which could have challenged the older parties. In 1964, Jallow became the full time Secretary-General of the African Regional Office of the International Confederation of Free Trade Unions with headquarters at Lagos.

JAM. A Wolof word for non-freeborn persons. Slaves in Wolof society belonged to one of two groups--those born in captivity and those captured in war. Although some slaves held high positions and most were treated well, they were always considered to be the property of the master who could do with them what he wished.

JAMBUR. A title in Wolof areas denoting freeborn persons.
   The freeborn were divided into three categories--those
   belonging to royal lineages, nobles not of such lineages,
   and the badolo (peasants), who made up the bulk of the
   population in a Wolof state.

JARRA. One of the nine Mandingo kingdoms located along
   the south bank of the Gambia River in the early 19th century. It joined Kiang on the west and extended eastward
   to Sofancama Bolon. During the latter stages of the
   Soninke-Marabout Wars much of Jarra was controlled by
   the powerful Marabout leader, Fodi Kabba. Because of
   the antipathy between Fodi Kabba and Musa Molloh, the
   area of eastern Jarra became a particular arena of conflict. In the 20th-century reorganization of the Protectorate, Jarra became a part of the Central Division and
   was divided into three districts, each under the direction
   of a chief.

JATTA, SULING. The king of Kombo who in 1840 was pressured by Lieutenant-Governor Huntley to cede to Britain
   a part of his kingdom for the payment of $100 which after-
   ward became known as British Kombo or Kombo St. Mary.
   This area was enlarged by a later cession in 1853 and
   gave the British approximately twenty-five square miles
   of land adjoining St. Mary's Island. Suling Jatta re-
   nounced his right to collect customs duties and rents in
   the ceded territory in 1850 in consideration of a small
   annual payment. His kingdom was one of the first Gambian areas to be struck by Islamic proselytizers. These
   Marabouts were particularly strong in Gunjur and Sabaji
   (Sukuta). By the end of 1851, it was apparent that Suling
   Jatta was losing much of his support to the preaching and
   raiding of the Muslims. Governor MacDonnell tried to per-
   suade the Colonial Office to take much of Kombo under
   British protection and thus bring an end to the internecine struggle. He was only authorized to seek a cession
   of a small strip of land from the king to add to British
   Kombo. This included the town of Sabaji, most of whose
   elders were Soninke, but the bulk of the population was
   loyal to the Marabouts. After much consideration, Suling
   Jatta agreed to the cession in May 1853. The townspeople
   of Sabaji refused to accept the agreement, and British
   forces took the town by storm in 1853. This was not the
   end of the affair since the Marabout leaders, Omar and

Fodi Kabba, launched an attack in June 1855 against both
Suling Jatta and British Kombo. The Marabouts almost
succeeded in taking Bathurst. Marabouts from Gunjur
tried to take Busumballa, the king's town. The attack
was beaten off, but Suling Jatta was killed. The ensuing
struggle for power between the Soninke families of Yundum and Busumballa over the succession greatly helped
the Kombo Marabouts in their bid for power.

JAWARA. The title given to a general appointed to command
the armies in a Mandingo state.

JAWARA, SIR DAUDA KAIRABA. Prime Minister of the Gambia from 1962 to 1970 and President of the Republic since
its inception in 1970. He was born in the Protectorate at
Barajally in 1924. His father, a prosperous Mandinka
farmer, chose him from among his six sons to be educated
at Bathurst, first at the Muslim primary school, then later
at the Methodist Boys High School. After graduation in
1945, he worked at the Royal Victoria Hospital and won a
scholarship to Achimota College and later attended the
Veterinary School at Glasgow University where he qualified as a veterinary surgeon. In the 1950s, he gained a
further diploma in tropical veterinary medicine. In 1954,
he returned to the Gambia and became a veterinary officer in the Protectorate. In 1955, he was converted to
Christianity and married Augusta, a daughter of Sir John
Mahoney, one of the leaders of the Aku community in
Bathurst. They had five children before their divorce
in 1967. He subsequently married the present Lady Jawara.

In 1965, Jawara reverted to Islam and changed his
name from David to Dauda. He helped form the People's
Progressive Party in 1959 and was chosen its leader. In
the elections of 1960, the PPP elected nine representatives
to the House as compared to the opposition United Party's
seven, and Jawara served briefly as Minister of Education.
However, he and all the PPP ministers resigned when the
governor appointed P. S. N'Jie of the United Party as
Chief Minister. In the elections of 1962, Jawara's party
won an overwhelming victory and he became Prime Minister. His government cooperated fully with the governor
and the Colonial Office in negotiating the constitutional
instruments of an independent Gambia. When the Gambia
became independent on February 18, 1965, Jawara continued

as Prime Minister. As such, he was responsible for the increasing solvency of the government and for continuing
an evolutionary program of closer cooperation with Senegal. He was knighted in 1966. Jawara's proposal to convert the Gambia to a Republic was rejected by the voters
in 1965 by only 700 votes. However, when resubmitted
to the electorate in April 1970, the change was overwhelm-
ingly approved. On April 24, Jawara became the first
President of the Republic of the Gambia.

In the subsequent elections in 1977 and 1982 Jawara
was reelected by huge majorities over his opponent, Sheriff Dibba of the National Convention Party. The PPP in
both elections won over 70 percent of the popular vote
thus totally dominating the legislature. During the 1970s
despite Gambia's relative unimportance, Jawara emerged
as an articulate spokesman for moderation and an opponent of radical Islamic solutions. He was also active in
calling the world's attention to the problem of the environ-
ment and the need for conservation of Africa's resources.
In 1980 he was awarded the Agricolan medal by the FAO
of the United Nations for his untiring efforts to bring relief to the drought-stricken sahel. Although the Gambia was more fortunate than many of its neighbors, the
continuing drought adversely affected agricultural production in the middle and upper river areas and seriously
threatened Gambia's hard won economic independence.

The first half-decade of the 1980s witnessed even more
controlled expenditures and forced Jawara's government to
borrow to meet the recurrent budget. These economic
problems led to the attempt to oust the President and his
party by force. In July 1981, while Jawara was in Britain,
disaffected radicals seized power briefly in Banjul. Flying
to Senegal, Jawara invoked the 1967 defense treaty between
the two states. Supported by elements of the Senegalese
army, he returned to a shattered Banjul where the loss of
life during the abortive coup attempt amounted to over 600
persons. This tragedy led to closer relations with Senegal
and the conclusion in late 1981 of the Confederation of
Senegambia. Although much remained to be done to fully
implement this agreement, President Jawara in his capacity
as Vice-President of the Confederation continued to en-
courage the slow cautious movement toward the integration
of the two states.

JIHAD. According to Muslim theology, taking up the sword

either in defense of or to expand the true faith was the obligation of every believer. He should resort to violence only after persuasion and argumentation has failed. The term "jihad," originally Arabic, is found in all the Senegambian languages. The first major jihads in West Africa were those of the Almoravids of the 11th century. From that time forward there were many aimed at spreading the influence of Islam. Any war undertaken against non-Muslims was likely to be pursued as if it were a jihad, although technically most were not. The most notable of the 19th-century jihads in Senegambia were those led by Al Hajj Umar and the Soninke-Marabout wars, which ravaged the areas adjacent to the Gambia River for over half a century.

JIMARA. One of the nine Mandingo kingdoms located along the south bank of the Gambia River in the early 19th century. It was one of the larger and more prosperous of the upriver polities and had a long history of trade with Europeans since MacCarthy Island was located adjacent to the middle areas of Jimara. Alfa Molloh was a resident of Jimara and it was there that he made his first conquest, overthrowing the traditional Mandingo dynasty. Jimara became the nucleus of his new kingdom of Fuladu. In the 20th-century reorganization of the chiefdoms, the area which was Jimara became the Districts of Fuladu West and Fuladu Central.

JOAR. A village on the north bank of the mid-Gambia River which was the site of a number of trade factories established by the Portuguese and later English trading companies. The English had factories there in 1704 and between 1723 and 1727. The Royal African Company post there in the 1730s was their principal out factory on the river.

JOB BEN SOLOMON (Job Jallow). Son of a Fulbe ruler in Bondu. In the early 18th century he was captured in the Gambia and sold into slavery. Job was transported to Maryland where he labored for over a year. Fortunately, one of his letters, written to his father in Arabic, fell into the hands of General Oglethorpe who was so impressed that he ransomed him. Job then began a 14-month stay in Britain where he assisted Sir Hans Sloane with Arabic translations and was presented at the court of George II. Agents of the Royal African Company were ordered to treat him with great respect when he returned to the Gambia in 1734. He and Francis Moore became good friends and Job accompanied Moore on a number of travels to trading stations before returning to Bondu in 1736 with a company servant, Thomas Hull. Job was responsible for interceding with one of his patrons, the Duke of Montagu, to free a friend, Lahmin Jay, from slavery in Maryland. Jay, after returning to Gambia, joined Job in Bondu. The last record of Job dates to 1740 when he came to James Island and led a company agent, Melchior de Jaspas, back to Bondu.

JOBSON, RICHARD. A supercargo for the English Guinea Company who arrived with two ships and much trade goods in the Gambia in 1620. After seizing property from local Portuguese inhabitants in reprisal for their looting and subsequent massacre of the crew of an English ship, Jobson's ships proceeded to Tendeba. Jobson took one of the ships to Mangegar, where a house was purchased from the chief which was to be used as a trading factory. It was decided that Jobson with seven men should continue the exploration of the river. He reached Barrakunda Falls in January 1621, and Tenda the following month. He made friends with the local rulers, discovered the nature and type of trade to be had in the upper river, and found that the Portuguese were no longer a force on the river. By the time that Jobson returned to his ships, disease had reduced the complement to such an extent that Jobson left the Gambia in May. He was convinced of the wealth which could be obtained by trading in the Gambia and labored hard to convince the English Royal family to subsidize further ventures. One of the propaganda weapons he used was his book on the expedition entitled The Golden Trade. In 1624, he was entrusted with command of another expedition to the Gambia but the venture was a failure. A later book, The Discovery of the Country of King Solomon, did not further influence English sponsors, but played an important role in spurring French interest in the Senegambia. The French formed a company in 1626 to exploit the river trade. Jobson, however, never returned to the Gambia.

JOINER, THOMAS. A Mandinka merchant who, in the early 19th century, became one of the most affluent Bathurst

traders. He had been a griot as a young man, but was
captured and sold into slavery in one of the southern
United States. There he learned the craft of carpentry
(which probably gave him his name). He was fortunate
to be able to purchase his freedom and, in about 1805,
had returned to the Gambia. Beginning with only a small
amount of money, he had, by trading with the upper
river areas, become wealthy even before the town of
Bathurst was begun. Joiner owned a number of ships
and boats engaged in the river trade among which was
the largest craft operating from the port of Bathurst.
His ships made regular journeys with passengers and
cargo to Sierra Leone, the Cape Verdes, the Isles de
Los, and the Madeiras. At one time he employed over
100 persons to help carry on his trading activities.
Joiner considered himself, and was so considered, a
prominent member of the largely European trading community of Senegambia. He had become by the time of
his death in 1842 the most respected Gambian trader in
Bathurst.

JOKADU. One of the five Mandingo controlled kingdoms on
the north bank of the Gambia River in the early 19th
century, bounded on the west by Jurunku Bolon and on
the east by Kutang Bolon. In 1862, the area was captured by Amer Faal, one of Ma Bâ's lieutenants, and the
people were forced to accept Islam. It was then incorporated into Ma Bâ's kingdom of Baddibu (Rip) and its
history in the latter years of the century was bound to
the struggles for control of this larger state by the successors of Ma Bâ. The chieftaincy was restored by the
British reorganization of the Protectorate in the 20th century when it became a District in the Lower River Division.

JOLAS. Comprise approximately 10 percent of the population
of the Gambia with the majority (approximately 20,000) re-
siding in the Foni areas south of Bintang Bolon. Some
Jola traditions suggest a common origin for themselves and
the Serer in the upper Gambia region. They still maintain
a joking relationship with the Serer. It is probable that
the Jolas are the people longest resident in the Gambia region and were overcome by a series of Mandingo invasions.
Some of the earliest European visitors mention the Jola,
whom they called Feloops, living in the same locales where
they now live. Their political and social organization was

village oriented and not as sophisticated as those of the
Mandingo or Wolof. Moore and Park both reported in the
18th century that although the Jola paid tribute to their
Mandingo overlords, they had not been completely subju-
gated and continued to exercise great freedom. The Jola
were noted for their competence in war. A number of
times in the 18th century the Jola came to the assistance
of British traders and soldiers during conflicts with the
French. In the latter 19th century many Jola served as
mercenaries in the Soninke-Marabout Wars. Disdaining
the religious position of both Muslims and Mandingo, they
served both sides. However, they strongly resisted the
attempts by Fodi Kabba to convert them to Islam. In 1887,
the chiefs of 16 Jola towns signed a treaty with Sir Samuel
Rowe at Kansala whereby they placed themselves under
British protection.

JOLOF. The original of the Wolof states, it was formed before the 14th century. Its rise was probably occasioned
by the breakup of the kingdom of Tekrur and the demise
of Malian power in the Senegambia region. The Wolof
probably migrated from Tekrur into most parts of what is
now Senegal. Eventually by the 16th century, five major
states--Walo, Cayor, Baol, Sine, and Saloum--owed allegiance to the ruler (burba) of Jolof. In the course of the
following century all of these revolted against Jolof domination and the state became relatively isolated from the
lucrative trade with Europeans. Because of its location,
it was open to attacks from Mauritania and by the more
prosperous coastal states of Cayor, Walo, and Baol. Much
of the population was early converted to Islam. In the
Soninke-Marabout Wars, Jolof was conquered by Ma Bâ's
forces and briefly became a part of the kingdom of Rip.
The Burba Jolof in the 1880s allied himself with the faction supporting Saër Maty in Baddibu. The use of Jolof
for raids into French protected areas led to a French expedition in 1890 and its subsequent absorption into the
French empire.

JOLOF TOWN. A section of Banjul (Bathurst) adjacent to
Soldier Town and Half Die fronting on Wellington Street,
and is sometimes called Melville Town. It is today the
site of most of the major trading and business establishments. In the early 19th century this section of the city
was largely inhabited by Wolof artisans.

JONES, SAMUEL H. M. Educator and government official,
    born of an Aku family in Bathurst in 1923. He was edu-
    cated at the Bathurst Methodist Boys High School, Achi-
    mota, Exeter University, and the London Institute of Ed-
    ucation. From 1944 to 1947, he taught in the Gambian
    primary schools. In 1952, he became the assistant master
    of his old high school where he remained until entering
    government service as an education officer in 1960. In
    the 1950s he was the president of the Gambia Teachers
    Union and a representative on the West African Examina-
    tions Council. He was seconded to the World Confedera-
    tion of Organizations of the Teaching Profession in 1960,
    travelled extensively throughout Africa, and produced a
    report for them on the status of teaching in Africa. In
    1962, he returned briefly to the Gambian Ministry of Edu-
    cation before being posted as Liaison Officer to the Gam-
    bia Office in London. Later he became Commissioner when
    the name of the office was changed.

JONES, SAMUEL HORTON OLUWALE. A medical practitioner,
    born in 1909 and educated at the Methodist Boys High
    School. In 1925, he transferred to the Church Missionary
    Society Grammar School in Freetown and after completion
    of work there in 1928, attended Manchester University,
    receiving his degree in 1934. He then attended the Lon-
    don School of Tropical Hygiene and Medicine and became
    a Medical Officer in the Gambia in 1936. He was promoted
    to Senior Medical Officer in 1951, and became the Director
    of Medical Services in the following year, a post he held
    until retirement in 1964.

JONGO. The title given in Mandingo society to the slaves,
    comparable to the Wolof jam.

JUFFURE. A Mandingo village on the north bank of the
    Gambia River opposite James Island. In the early 18th
    century there was also a large number of half-caste
    Portuguese residents there. The English maintained fac-
    tories there for a century after 1680. At first these were
    sponsored by the large chartered companies, but later
    were maintained by independent traders. In the early
    18th century, Juffure provided the garrison at Fort James
    with a large portion of their vegetable requirements.
        Juffure gained considerable prominence in the 1970s
    because the American author Alex Haley claimed that this

was the village of his ancestor Kunta Kinte in the very
popular semi-fictional book Roots. Because of this work
Juffure became the center of a short-lived tourist boom.

JULA. Mandinka word for a trader. It has also come to de-
note a number of related groups of Mandinka of merchant
origin who settled along the major trading routes in the
Western Sudan, Sierra Leone, Guinea, and the Gambia.

JUNJUN. A small drum approximately 2½ feet long used by
the Wolof only to announce the arrival of chiefs. It is
beaten by a curved stick, only one hand being used by
the drummer.

JUSTOBAQUE, PETER. The factor of the (Dutch) West Indies Company at Goree who in mid-1661 attempted to oust
the British from their newly won superiority in trade on
the Gambia River. Sailing up the Gambia River, he partly
neutralized the small British garrison at Charles Fort on
Dog Island. However, he was thwarted by the firm action
of the British factor at James Fort who refused all Justobaque's arguments, promises of reward, and threats. Finally, Justobaque withdrew from the river and the directors of the Dutch company and the States General took no
further immediate action to drive the English from the
Gambia.

-K-

KABILO-TIYO. In Mandingo kingdoms, the kabilo-tiyo was
in charge of a kabilo or a collection of yards. He was
normally the senior man of a particular lineage.

KAH, KEBBA A. H. Teacher and politician born to an Islamic Wolof family at Medina Mas Kah in the Protectorate
in 1934. He was educated in Koranic schools, the Catholic mission school, and the Teachers Training College.
Kah taught at a number of Protectorate schools until he
resigned to enter politics in 1959. He was at first affili-
ated with the United Party and was elected to the Assembly in 1960. When P. S. N'Jie became Chief Minister, Kah
was appointed to head the Ministry of Health. After the
1962 election, he changed his affiliation to the People's
Progressive Party and was appointed to head the Ministry

of Finance and later that of Works and Communication before being chosen to serve as Minister of Health in 1965.

KANTORA. The uppermost of the Mandingo controlled kingdoms lying on the south bank of the Gambia River. The
rulers and traders of Kantora are mentioned in 15th-
century Portuguese accounts because of their alleged
possession of great quantities of gold. Kantora was one
of the Mandingo states which the Mollohs attempted to
absorb into Fuladu during the Soninke-Marabout conflicts
in the 1870s. Although they were never completely successful, the older traditional rule in Kantora was broken.
In the British reorganization of the chiefdoms of the Gambia in the 20th century, the area of the ancient kingdom
and its name was revived as a District in the Upper River
Division.

KEMINTANG. A Soninke chief who in the 1820s was contest-
ing with Kolli, the chief of Kataba, for the overlordship
of Niani. The power relationships were partially upset by
Kolli's ceding the Island of Lemain (MacCarthy Island) to
the British in 1823. But the British could not maintain a
force large enough on the island to bring peace to the
adjoining areas, and the endemic warfare continued. In
1834, a dispute arose between Kemintang and a Bathurst
merchant at Tendeba, and Kemintang seized a vessel belonging to another merchant and held it for ransom until
the British would redress the wrongs he had suffered. Instead, Lieutenant-Governor Rendall declared an embargo
on upper river trade and in August dispatched a 120-man
force against the chief. Kemintang retired to Dungaseen,
a fortified town near the headwaters of Sami Creek. The
invaders dragged their cannon and ammunition through 20
miles of sand and mud only to find the walls of the town
impervious to artillery. Abandoning the guns, two of
which could still be used, they retreated to the Gambia
River. Kemintang mounted these guns on the walls of his
town, and his victory gave him added prestige in Niumi.
Despite a number of British efforts, he refused to surrender the artillery, and continued to make sporadic war
against Kataba until his death in 1843.

KENNEDY, SIR ARTHUR. Appointed Governor of the Gambia
in 1851, but never took up the post. Between 1852 and
1854, he administered the Colony of Sierra Leone, and in

1868 he was appointed Governor of the West African Settlements and became one of the key figures in the negotiations for the exchange of British possessions in the
Gambia for French territory elsewhere. The Colonial Office, responding to French offers, ordered Kennedy to
investigate and report on the situation in the Gambia. In
1869, he visited Bathurst for the first time and spent 10
days in the Gambia. Thus the detailed reports on conditions in the territory submitted to the Colonial Office during the following six years were not based on personal
observation or detailed knowledge, but on reports from
subordinates and merchants who did have experience of
Gambian conditions. Despite this obvious lack of first-
hand knowledge, the Colonial Office viewed Kennedy as
their expert. Even before his visit to Bathurst, Kennedy
was in favor of some exchange that would consolidate West
African territories claimed by both nations. Kennedy
further argued that the Gambia was a useless appendage
which cost Britain in military expenditures more than the
territory was worth. What trade there was, was in the
hands of French merchants, and the "peculiar population"
was resistant to all attempts to extend civilization to the
areas outside the Colony. Kennedy's first long reports
along with similar ones from the administrator, Rear Admiral Patey, convinced the British government to propose
to France a sweeping exchange of territory. By March
1870, all the details of the exchange had been worked out
except the rights of English and French subjects in the
ceded territories. However, the Franco-Prussian War in-
terrupted the negotiations for exchange and discussions
were not resumed until 1875. Kennedy left West Africa in
1872.

KËR. Wolof word for house. It can also mean a compound
or, in a broader connotation, an extended family, a lineage, or the village of an important person.

KESSELLIKUNDA. A town in Fuladu which was the residence
of Musa Molloh after his movement in 1903 from the Casamance into British territory. The British recognized Musa
Molloh's position as head of British Fuladu and paid him a
handsome stipend until they could no longer ignore his
practice of slavery and rumored atrocities. In 1919, they
pulled down his compound at Kessillikunda and exiled Musa
to Sierra Leone.

KHALIFA. Wolof and Fulbe title for the leader of a community of believers. The term was originally Arabic and was
among the many borrowed by West Africans. In Wolof the
term is normally applied to the head of a brotherhood or
one of its branches.

KIANG. One of the nine Mandingo kingdoms located along the
south bank of the Gambia River in the early 19th century.
It stretched from the juncture of Bintang Bolon and the
Gambia River eastward to a point opposite Devils Point.
Bintang Bolon separated Kiang from Foni on the south.
The major port towns of Tankular and Tendeba are in
Kiang. Because of its location and wealth, Kiang was a
major prize in the Soninke-Marabout conflicts. Ma Bâ's
attempt to gain a firm foothold on the south bank was
thwarted at Quinella in Kiang. Eastern Kiang by the
1870s was firmly controlled by Fodi Kabba while the central and western parts were still in the hands of the
Soninke or owed allegiance to Fodi Silla. Kiang continued
to be an area of disorder until after the killing of Travelling Commissioners Sitwell and Wilva and a large part of
their force at Sankandi in 1900. After the British reorganization of the Protectorate in the 20th century, Kiang
was placed in the Central Division and divided into three
Districts, each under the direction of a chief.

KILHAM, HANNAH. A member of the Society of Friends who
in 1823 arrived in the Gambia as the leader of one of the
first industrial missionary endeavors sent to Africa. The
two European men of this group started an agricultural
school at Cape St. Mary while Mrs. Kilham and another
woman, Anne Thompson, opened a school for girls in
Bathurst. Later a Wesleyan missionary arrived in the
Gambia and Mrs. Kilham turned her school over to them
and took up residence in Bakau where she opened another girls' school. Within a few months all the members
of the Friend's mission were stricken with fever and were
forced to return to England, thus ending the Quaker experiment in Westernized technical education.

KING'S BOYS. Recaptive slaves who had served with the
Royal African Corps and the West Indian Regiments and
had been pensioned or discharged. They were the first
of the Liberated Africans to be sent to the Gambia. Beginning in the early 1820s, a number of these ex-soldiers

settled along Oyster Creek with grants of land and free
farming implements. Some of the King's Boys became
government ferrymen, others burned lime from the oyster
shells for the Bathurst market, and still others found em-
ployment in the construction of the first public buildings
in Bathurst.

KOMBO. One of the traditional south bank Mandingo kingdoms. The rulers of Kombo controlled the lands adjacent
to the mouth of the Gambia River. The peoples of Kombo
had long been in contact with Europeans because of its
location. Captain Grant purchased St. Mary's Island on
which to build the town of Bathurst (Banjul) from the
king of Kombo. The price was an annual payment of 103
iron bars (approximately £25). Later in 1853, the British
negotiated a further cession of land from Suling Jatta,
another ruler of Kombo. This new area became British
Kombo, and the transaction helped to precipitate the
Soninke-Marabout conflict in the lower river territories.
The wars began in the Kombo with the activities of Omar
of Sabaji and Fodi Kabba. The greatest threat to the
continued British presence on the river came from the
warfare between the contending factions in Kombo in the
mid-1850s. The problem was not resolved until 1855 when
Suling Jatta was killed and the Marabouts loyal to Fodi
Kabba controlled western Kombo.

KONKO. A short handled adze-shaped tool that is used for
planting peanuts. The sower uses the konko in one hand
to make holes in the ground while with the other hand he
drops the seeds into the holes.

KORDU-TIYO. The Protectorate Ordinance of 1902 and all
those which followed until 1933 accepted the yard as the
basic political institution throughout the Gambia. A yard
was defined as a collection of several huts which had at
one time been held by a kindred grouping. The head of
a yard was normally referred to by the Mandingo term
kordu-tiyo. These local leaders were each under the
supervision of the village head called the satiyo-tiyo.

KORTRIGHT, SIR CORNELIUS H. Administrator of the
Gambia from 1873 to 1875 who was deeply involved in the
1974-76 Colonial Office plans to cede the Gambia to France.
He acted as the chief source for the Colonial Office

planners. His report that Bathurst mercantile opinion would not be hostile if proper compensation was paid proved to be wrong since opposition from this section became very organized and vocal. Kortright was promoted to Governor of the British West African Settlements (Sierra Leone and the Gambia) in 1875 and held this post for two years.

KOTO, MANSA. The chief of Battelling whose town was selected by Travelling Commissioner F. C. Sitwell in 1900 as the neutral ground to adjudicate the quarrel between Marabouts and Soninkes in Kiang. When Dari Bana Dabo, the Marabout leader of Sankandi, refused to parley, Mansa Koto and some of his retainers accompanied Sitwell and his party to Sankandi. When the people of Sankandi opened fire, Mansa Koto was killed along with the Travelling Commissioner and the bulk of the armed escort.

-L-

LAHAMIN JAY. A Mandingo-speaking Fulbe who had been captured, sold into slavery, and sent to Maryland with Job ben Solomon. Job, after his release, petitioned the Duke of Montagu to secure the release of Lahamin Jay who was returned to the Gambia by the Royal African Company in 1738. He became a part of the mission headed by Melchior de Jaspas in 1740 which sought to improve trade between the company and the kingdom of Bondu.

LAIDLEY, DR. JOHN. A surgeon who in 1791 joined Robert Aynsley, a trader, at his station at Pisania (Karantaba). He acted as the banker for Major Daniel Houghton and later Mungo Park in their expeditions into the western Sudan. Park spent the latter six months of 1795 at Laidley's house while studying Mandingo, and it was to Laidley's house that he returned after his successful exploration.

LAM; LAMAN. Wolof and Fulbe title for a chief. In some cases it refers to the original chief of a lineage.

LAMINE, MOMADU. A Muslim leader from Bondu who had contested French domination and was driven to take refuge at Toubacouta where he was welcomed by the son

of Simotto Moro. A French expedition followed Lamine to
the Gambia, and Musa Molloh, then an ally of the French,
crossed the Gambia River with a large army. The combined forces took Toubacouta in 1886 and Momadu Lamine,
according to legend, was killed by Musa.

LEBANESE. A minority group in the Senegambia comprising
    migrants from Lebanon and Syria. The first migrants
    began arriving in the latter years of the 19th century
    and continued unabated until the independence of Senegal
    and Gambia when pressures were brought to bear on the
    Lebanese community which deprived them of some of the
    privileges they had enjoyed under imperial rule. Their
    ascendency in middle-level business originally was due to
    the preferences given to them by the large European com-
    mercial firms rather than to their African competitors.
    Although their numbers and influence have decreased,
    they still are the dominant mid-level merchants and are
    also active in transport and wholesale commerce.

LEGISLATIVE COUNCIL. One of two councils utilized in
    British colonies to assist the governor in making deci-
    sions. The small nominated Gambian Legislative Council
    was first created in 1843. When the Gambia was made
    dependent on Sierra Leone in 1866, its council was abol-
    ished only to be reestablished after the Gambia was
    constituted a separate colony in 1888. In 1893, the au-
    thority of the Council to make rules and orders was ex-
    tended to the Protectorate. In 1915, the Council was
    enlarged to include four official and three nominated
    unofficial members. In 1932, its size was increased by
    an additional African member nominated by the Urban
    District Council and by one of the Commissioners from
    the Protectorate. The Council was reorganized in 1947
    to contain three ex-officio members, three nominated
    government officials, six unofficial nominated members,
    and one elected member from Bathurst. In 1951 the
    number of elected members was increased to two. By
    the constitutional revision of 1954, there were five ex-
    officio official members, two nominated officials, seven
    directly elected members from the Colony, and seven
    indirectly elected from the Protectorate. After 1954,
    certain elected members were appointed to the Executive
    Council and allowed a share in directing the affairs of
    the government departments. Although they were not

yet really responsible, this was the necessary first step
toward ministerial government. According to the Constitution of 1960, the legislative instrument for the Gambia was
renamed the House of Representatives.

LEMAIN ISLAND. An important trading site for trans-Gambian
trade from areas in Senegal to the north as well as from
the upper Casamance. Europeans had maintained temporary trading stations on the island since Jobson's time.
In 1823, the British gained possession of Lemain Island
and renamed it MacCarthy Island in honor of the governor-
in-chief of the British West African Territories.

LIBERATED AFRICANS. Africans in transit as slaves to the
new world who were liberated, normally by warships of
the British West African Patrol. Because they were taken
twice, the term Recaptive came to be used to describe
these Africans. Most of the recaptives were taken to
Freetown, although they came from various parts of West
Africa and represented many different tribes and cultural
groups. They presented a considerable problem to the
British government in Freetown which had only limited
funds available for resettlement. Many of the recaptives
in the 1820s and 1830s found their way to the Gambia
where they became the nucleus of a Westernized population in Bathurst. The Akus (Yoruba) became particularly important in trade and commerce, and their descendants
were among the first to occupy important posts in the civil
service and government of 20th-century Gambia.

LLEWELLYN, SIR RICHARD B. Administrator of the Gambia,
1891-1901. He was the man most responsible for establishing the early forms of Indirect Rule in the Protectorate.
British control over most of the Gambia River areas after
the Convention of 1889 had been exercised in an ad hoc
intermittent manner until 1893 when Llewellyn appointed
the first Travelling Commissioner. After months of study
of other British Colonial dependencies, particularly India,
the governor and his staff issued the Protectorate Ordinance of 1894. Later governors modified this legislation,
but the basic form and mechanics of Protectorate government as stated in the 1894 Ordinance remained in effect
until the eve of Gambian independence. Llewellyn was
also primarily responsible for modifying the more extreme
demands of the French representatives on the various

boundary commissions of the 1890s. He and his advisors
drew up and instituted the plans for the joint operation
with the French in 1901 which finally destroyed the influence of Fodi Kabba.

-M-

MCP   see   MUSLIM CONGRESS PARTY

MacCARTHY, SIR CHARLES.   Governor-in-Chief of the British West African Territories (1814-1824) who made the
recommendation to the Colonial Office in 1815 that Britain
reoccupy James Island. He supported Captain Alexander
Grant in his decision not to attempt the rebuilding of the
fort on the island, but rather to purchase Banjul (St.
Mary's) Island from the king of Kombo and build the
British base there. Although until 1821 the government
of the Gambia was military and seemingly of a temporary
nature, MacCarthy had enlisted the support of the newly
arrived Bathurst merchants for the government, and he
had established a courts system. After 1821, the Gambia
was officially made a part of the British West African Territories he controlled from his headquarters in Freetown.
In 1824, MacCarthy was killed at Bonsaso in the Gold Coast
while leading his troops in an abortive invasion of Ashanti-
land. MacCarthy Island was subsequently named for him.

MacCARTHY ISLAND.   Called Lemain Island in the 18th century, it was the site of temporary trading stations from
the time of Jobson. In 1823, the British took possession
of the island and despite much pressure from the Soninke-
Marabout Wars and a penurious treasury, it remained
throughout the century their chief enclave in the interior.
Georgetown, one of the larger towns of the interior, is
located on the island.

MacDONNELL, SIR RICHARD GRAVES.   Governor of the
Gambia from 1847 until early 1852. In 1844 while serving
as first Chief Justice of the Colony, he made one of the
longest journeys into the hinterland seeking information
on the people, their customs, and potential trade. He
travelled by water to Fattatenda where he met three
Frenchmen who had just visited Bondu. From Fattatenda
he travelled on foot to the capital of Bondu where he

induced the ruler to repudiate the exclusive trade treaty
he had just made with the Frenchmen, and extracted a
promise that the route from Bondu to the Gambia River
would be kept open. After being appointed governor,
MacDonnell in 1849 and 1850 undertook yet other explorations. In 1849 he travelled by boat over 100 miles beyond
Barrakunda Falls. In the following year he reached Jalla-
kotta on the Neriko River. He was disappointed by both
expeditions since he found the river above the falls difficult to navigate, the country sparsely settled, and little
sign of major cultivation of any exportable crop. On the
return journey in 1850, Governor MacDonnell's party narrowly escaped death when he visited Kunnong near Quinella.
The inhabitants of Kunnong, after driving off MacDonnell,
then pillaged a trading post nearby. On his return to
Bathurst, MacDonnell organized a punitive expedition which
eventually forced the chief of Kunnong to signify his sub-
mission to the British governor. Earlier in 1849, MacDonnell had helped organize a joint French-British expedition
against the Papels on Bissago Island who had made a practice of capturing shipwrecked vessels and their crews.

MacNAMARA, MATTHIAS. An Ensign in O'Hara's Corps in
the Senegambia who was selected over senior officers to
be Lieutenant-Governor at James Island in 1774. He dis-
obeyed orders, seized French trading ships, and traded
privately with the Africans. Despite such actions, he
became the Governor of Senegambia in late 1775. Almost
immediately he began a quarrel with Captain Wall who had
taken his place at James Island. MacNamara ordered Wall's
arrest and kept him in confinement for ten months at the
fort before bringing him to trial. Wall was subsequently
cleared of the charges and in two civil suits won damages
from MacNamara who was removed as Governor of Senegambia by the Council of Trade in August 1778.

MAHONEY, SIR JOHN. One of the leaders of the Bathurst
community in the Second quarter of the 20th century. He
was the recognized leader of the Mahoney family which
counted some of the most educated and influential people
in Bathurst. Some of these were the lawyer Jacob Mahoney, the eventual Minister of Health, John Mahoney and
his wife, Florence, the first Gambian Ph.D., and Augusta,
the first wife of Prime Minister Jawara. Sir John was a
longtime friend of Edward Small and other early nationalists,

and in the 1940s was a nominated member of the Legislative Council. In the early 1950s, he became the Speaker
of the Legislative Council, and just before his retirement,
he was named the Speaker of the House of Representatives
in 1960.

MALI EMPIRE. After the Almoravids overthrew the kingdom
of Ghana in the 11th century, there ensued a century and
a half of military and commercial rivalry between a number
of powerful city states of the western Sudan. Eventually
in the 13th century, the Mandingo ruler Sundiata defeated
his Soso rivals. On the base of Sundiata's conquest, later
rulers built the Malian empire, the most powerful and rich-
est empire ever developed in the Sudan. It reached its
apex under Mansa Musa in the 14th century, its fame being underscored by Mansa Musa's legendary trip to Mecca.
Before its downfall, the empire included eastern Senegal,
and many Gambian riverine rulers paid homage and tribute
to the great king of Mali.

MALTA PLAN. In the late 1950s, this was one solution suggested for small British dependencies which were considered to be too weak or economically nonviable to become
totally independent. It was at first proposed to solve the
problem of the island of Malta, and was also proposed for
the Gambia. The chief feature of the plan was some type
of federal association between the dependent territories
and Great Britain. With the political leaders of most of
the smaller areas opting for independence, the plan was
abandoned even before details of association were seriously discussed.

MANDINGO. One of the most important people resident in
the Gambia. In present-day Gambia, they comprise over
40 percent of the estimated population. The Mandingo are
spread fairly evenly throughout the length of the country.
The Gambian Mandingo are the most westerly extension of
the Manding group of people who speak kindred languages
of the northern sub-group of the Niger-Congo family of
languages and have similar political and social organizations. Some of the other West African Manding speakers
are the Bambara, Dyula, and Kuranko. The Mandingo
people are long resident in the Gambia, probably moving
into the area during the period of disorder in the western
Sudan following the breakup of the empire of Ghana in the

11th century. Richard Jobson noted in the 17th century
that Mandingo rulers in the Gambia still showed deference
to the ruler of Mali long after the breakdown of its hegemony over the western Sudan. Mandingo society was divided into three endogamous castes--the freeborn (foro),
slaves (jongo), and artisans or praise singers (nyamalo).
Age groups (kafo) were important in Mandingo society in
contrast to the socio-political organizations of neighboring
Wolof people. The basis of life for the Mandingo was and
is agriculture, although they were also the dominant traders on the river. In the latter 19th century, cultivation
of peanuts became the major concern for most Mandingo
farmers.

In the 19th century almost all the riverine territories
of the Gambia were controlled by a number of Mandingo
rulers (mansa) through the medium of related but separate and competing kingdoms. These were Niumi, Jokadu,
Baddibu, Upper and Lower Niani, and Wuli on the north
bank, and Kombo, Foni, Kiang, Jarra, Niamina, Eropina,
Jimara, Tomani, and Kantora along the south bank. Rule
in each of these states was based upon kinship and each
king surrounded himself with his own complex bureaucracy. The kingdoms were subdivided into territorial units
of the village, ward, and family compound. Village administration was carried out by the satiyo-tiyo (alkali) in
council. Each village was further divided into kabilos or
wards which were administered by a kabilo-tiyo. Each of
these officials was chosen on a basis of his lineage as well
as his abilities. The kings each maintained an armed
force to defend the state and impose their will on their
subjects. Since they were not permitted to lead troops,
the rulers chose a general (jawara) for this function.
The Mandingo systems of rule were challenged in the latter 19th century by proselytizing teachers who wished to
convert the Mandingo to Islam. The conflicts which ensued led to the half century series of wars called the
Soninke-Marabout Wars which resulted in the conversion
of most of the people to Islam and a breakdown of traditional Mandingo authority structures in the Gambia.

MANE, KOLLIMANKE. King of Barra at the time when
Alexander Grant began the construction of the first buildings in Bathurst. The king allowed the British to quarry
stone on Dog Island and made no stipulation for direct
payment. Undoubtedly this was done because Grant in

1816 reordered the method of payment whereby the king
benefitted more directly from customs duties than previously. Nevertheless, after Kollimanke Mane's death in
1823, this incident was remembered by the new king and
his advisors, and was one of the latent reasons for the
Barra War of 1831.

MANSA. Mandingo title for the king of one of their traditional states.

MARABOUTS. Initially Muslim religious teachers who later
came to exercise considerable political and economic influence. At the court of every Senegambian ruler who
had accepted Islam, there would be at least one Marabout
whose responsibilities in normal times were to pray for
the ruler, give advice, and handle correspondence. In
the disturbed conditions after 1850, some of the Marabouts came to wield great political influence, and some
such as Ma Bâ became themselves the rulers of large
kingdoms. This was the case in many areas adjacent to
the Gambia River where traditional rulers and their en-
tourages refused to accept Islam. The series of civil
wars called the Soninke-Marabout Wars were initially based
on the desires of reforming Marabouts to overthrow the
"pagan" traditional rulers and convert the people to Islam.

M'BAKI, OMAR. Politician and former seyfu in Sami District.
One of the few educated chiefs in the Gambia in the late
1950s. He served for 14 years as a member of the Executive Council during British rule. After the election of
1960, he was a minister in the government of P. S. N'Jie
and was the spokesman for the indirectly elected Protectorate chiefs. At this time he was considered by some as a
political alternative to the leaders of the two major parties.
When the People's Progressive Party came to power, he
managed a compromise with Sir Dauda Jawara and the other
government leaders. However, in 1965 he and six other
chiefs were dismissed by the central government for anti-
government attitudes.

MEDICAL RESEARCH COUNCIL. One of the major African
tropical research units established at Fajara soon after
World War II and maintained by the Medical Research
Council of Great Britain and by Colonial Development

funds. Later a field station was established at Keneba.
A 40-bed research ward was maintained at Fajara. The
staff comprised a director, six medical and scientific officers, a number of expatriate staff, and over 75 Gambians.
The establishment was engaged in the study of tropical
diseases, particularly malaria, sickle cell anemia, and
filariasis. The facilities were regularly made available to
qualified visitors to carry out their own researches.

MOLLOH, ALFA   see   BALDE, ALFA MOLLOH EGUE

MOLLOH, MUSA   see   BALDE, MUSA MOLLOH

MOLONEY, CAPTAIN C. ALFRED. Administrator of the
Gambia from 1884 to 1885. His major contribution during
his brief tenure was the completion of the 300-yard-long
bridge over Oyster Creek.

MOORE, FRANCIS. Representative of the Royal African
Company and writer, who was sent to James Island in
1730. During his nearly five years stay in the Gambia,
Moore travelled throughout much of the area. He was a
trade factor in many places, most notably at Joar and
Yamyamacunda. Much of our knowledge of Gambian
social, economic, and political institutions in the 18th
century is due to Moore's keen interest in the riverine
Africans and their customs. His observations were published in 1735 in what became one of the classic books
detailing West African life, Travels in the Inland Parts
of Africa.

MUMBO JUMBO. Described by Francis Moore in the 18th
century as a figure of considerable importance in Mandingo society. He was a man dressed in leaves who was
called upon to judge the virtue of persons in a particular
village. He spoke a particular secret cant language not
understandable to women or outsiders. (The origin of
the English usage of the term.)

MUSLIM CONGRESS PARTY (MCP). The second political party
in the Gambia, it was formed from the Bathurst Young
Muslim Society and a number of smaller associations by
I. M. Garba-Jahumpa in January 1952. It sought to join
religious affiliation with political activity. In this, the
party was not successful, although individual members

did gain some political standing. Garba-Jahumpa in the
1950s continued to work closely with the Colonial government as a member of the Bathurst Town Council and as
one of the elected members of the Legislative Council. In
retrospect, this cooperation damaged the image of the Muslim Congress Party, and it became apparent before the
elections of 1960 that the United Party was likely to sweep
the elected seats in Bathurst. In order to obtain a broader support base, the leaders of the Muslim Congress Party
agreed in 1960 to merge their party with the Democratic
Party to form a new grouping called the Democratic Congress Alliance. After the failure of the DCA to become a
major factor in Gambian politics, Garba-Jahumpa led his
supporters into creating a new Congress Party. By 1968,
Garba-Jahumpa had settled his major differences with the
ruling People's Progressive Party, and the Congress Party
was disbanded.

-N-

NATIONAL CONVENTION PARTY (NCP). Formed by Sheriff
    Dibba, once a major force in the PPP, and a number of
    younger politicians dissatisfied with the style and sub-
    stance of PPP rule, the NCP soon emerged as the major
    opposition party in the Gambia. In the elections of 1977
    it gained over 40,000 votes and won five seats in the
    House of Representatives while the previous opposition,
    the United Party, was electing only two members. Dibba
    could gain only slightly more than 25 percent of the popu-
    lar vote for President. The chances of the NCP in the
    next election were seriously jeopardized when a number of
    its members were implicated in the attempted coup of 1981.
    Its leader, Sheriff Dibba, was imprisoned and was forced
    to direct his campaign for the presidency from his cell.
    Although later absolved from any wrongdoing, this was
    obviously one of the reasons for his crushing defeat by
    President Jawara in 1982. Nevertheless, the NCP sur-
    prisingly won three seats in the House and Dibba after
    his release continued to be the most important figure of
    all of the opponents of continued PPP rule.

NENYO. The caste to which the Wolof assigned artisans and
    various technicians. Smiths, leatherworkers, woodworkers,
    and the gewels or praise singers belong to this caste.

NIAMINA. One of the nine Mandingo-controlled kingdoms
   located along the south bank of the Gambia River in the
   early 19th century, located directly east and south of the
   river as it makes the great bend to the east. By the
   late 1870s, most of the traditional rulers had been driven
   out or had assumed a subordinate position to Fodi Kabba.
   Niamina was the most westerly extension of the kingdom
   of Fuladu, and therefore the eastern section was a battleground between the Marabout forces and those of the Mollohs'. During the 20th-century British reorganization of
   the Protectorate, Niamina was joined with the territory of
   the old Mandingo kingdom of Eropina. This composite was
   placed in the MacCarthy Island Division, then subdivided
   into three Districts, each under the direction of a chief.

NIANI. A north bank area which stretches from Nianiji Bolon
   on the west to Sandugu Bolon on the east. In the early
   19th century, this large territory was divided into two
   Mandingo-dominated kingdoms. In the 1830s, Kemintang
   caused considerable disturbance in the area and for a
   time dominated Upper Niani despite British attempts to
   defeat him. The ruler of Lower Niani whose base was at
   Kataba maintained excellent relations with the British in
   the 1840s, dating from the time when British military
   forces protected him from Kemintang. Despite the practice of allowing Marabouts a premier place in the kingdoms,
   Niani became a major battleground in the Soninke-Marabout
   Wars. Bounded on the west by Ma Bâ's kingdom of Baddibu (Rip) and on the east by Wuli, which was dominated
   by Bakari Sardu, the territory was ravaged by a series
   of competing armies. Later in the 1880s, the contending
   forces of Mamadou N'Dare and Saër Maty continued the
   unrest in Niani. Niani was divided into two Districts in
   the 20th-century British reorganization of the Protectorate. Upper Niani was renamed Sami. Each District was
   placed under the direction of a chief.

NIUMI. One of the five major north bank kingdoms controlled in the early 19th century by Mandingo rulers.
   Niumi was strategically located fronting on the Atlantic
   Ocean and dominating the entrance to the Gambia River.
   Because of its physical locale, Niumi was early in contact
   with the Europeans. In 1826, the British negotiated a
   treaty whereby the entire river frontage of Niumi passed
   to the British as the Ceded Mile. They proceeded

immediately to build Fort Bullen which would help command the entrance into the Gambia River. Difficulties
over this cession caused the Barra War of 1830-31. During the Soninke-Marabout Wars, Niumi was a major battleground, as first Ma Bâ and then his lieutenants sought to
add the territory to the kingdom of Rip (Baddibu). Amer
Faal was the most important of the Marabouts in Niumi who
from his base at Tubab Kolon continued to raid through
the area until a combined British and Soninke force took
his fortified town in 1866. Thereafter there was relative
peace in Niumi largely because the British considered the
security of Niumi vital for the maintenance of their authority in the Ceded Mile. In the 20th-century reorganization
of the Protectorate, the area became a District in the Lower
River Division and the ruler of Niumi was considered one
of the most important chiefs of the Protectorate.

N'JIE, ALHAJI A. B. Civil servant and politician, born of
a Wolof family in Bathurst in 1904. Although their names
are the same, he is not related to Pierre or Ebrimah N'Jie.
He attended Methodist mission schools in Bathurst and
entered the Civil Service in 1925. He held a number of
positions and retired in 1958 as the Registrar of the Supreme Court. Although a Muslim, he opposed the concept
held by the Muslim Congress of using religion for political
purposes, and instead helped form the Democratic Party.
He headed a number of ministries before being appointed
in the late 1960s as Minister of State for External Affairs
and Resident Minister in Dakar. In the reshuffle of the
ministry after Gambia became a Republic, he was made
Minister of Information, and in 1971 was appointed Minister of State at the President's Office.

N'JIE, EBRIMAH DOWDA. Lawyer, civil servant, and politician, and one of the founder members of the United
Party. Unlike his brother, Pierre Sarr N'Jie, Ebrimah
tended to stay in the background. Although a member
of the House of Representatives and a minister in his
brother's government of 1961, he did not aspire to high
office. He was a competent lawyer who devoted much of
his time to the law firm which he shared with his broth-
ers. A rift in the United Party in May 1970 caused the
party to depose P. S. N'Jie as leader and elect Ebrimah
to succeed him. However, before his leadership could
really be tested, he was killed in an automobile accident
in 1972.

N'JIE, PIERRE SARR. A Bathurst barrister and politician,
born July 17, 1909, and educated at St. Augustine's
School. While in his early twenties, he worked in a series of government departments including the Public Works
Department. He eventually became an assistant Clerk of
the Courts. In 1943, he left for England and served
briefly in the Royal Artillery. He began his legal training in 1944 at Lincoln's Inn and was called to the bar in
1948. He returned to the Gambia and began practicing
law in Bathurst. In 1951, he was defeated for an elected
seat on the Legislative Council. Shortly afterward, he
and other Wolof formed the United Party. In 1954, he
was elected to the Legislative Council at the head of the
poll. The following year he disagreed openly with Governor Wyn Harris and resigned from the government. His
absence from government proved fortunate since he escaped the stigma of appearing to be controlled by the
British. In the elections of 1960 for an expanded House
of Representatives, the United Party returned six members, although the newly formed People's Progressive
Party showed great popular strength in the Protectorate.
In 1961, because of his rapport with the Protectorate chiefs,
N'Jie was appointed Chief Minister. However, in the 1962
elections, the United Party could gain only 13 seats to the
PPP's 18 and P. S. N'Jie became the leader of the opposition. The influence of the United Party continued to decline after Gambian independence despite its power base
in the old Colony area and its coalitions with other Gambian parties. N'Jie's popularity also waned, and in May
1970, he was replaced as leader of the United Party by
his brother, E. D. N'Jie. After his brother's death in
1972, the party once more elected P. S. as leader. In
1973, his political fortunes reached a nadir when he was
removed from the roster of the House of Representatives
because of non-attendance.

NOHOR. Wolof term which distinguishes a person whose
father was dema but whose mother was not a witch. They
are believed to be gifted with second sight, but cannot
otherwise do harm.

NYAMALO. The title given in Mandingo society to the low-
born caste of artisans or praise singers, comparable to
the Wolof nenyo.

-O-

O'CONNOR, LUKE S. (COLONEL). Governor of the Gambia
from 1852 to 1859 and Commander in Chief of British military forces in West Africa. He recommended a forward
policy to the home government in order to secure Bathurst
and the Colony area from the threat of either the Marabouts or Soninke in adjacent areas. His suggestions were
not accepted, and he was forced to follow a defensive pos-
ture in regard to those leaders who threatened British
hegemony. He negotiated the cession of more territory
from Suling Jatta of Kombo and this helped precipitate
open conflict with Omar of Sabaji and Fodi Kabba of Gunjur. He sent a punitive expedition to Sabaji in 1853, but
this did not end the problem, and two years later, Omar
directed a major thrust at the Soninkes in Kombo and
their British protectors. In June 1855, O'Connor's forces
were defeated and he was wounded. Only by the most
strenuous efforts, and with the support of the king of
Barra and with French reinforcements from Senegal, was
he able to resume the offensive and capture Sabaji. In
April 1856, O'Connor arranged a truce between the Marabouts and Soninke in the Kombo. O'Connor was responsible for major additions to the town of Bathurst; he supervised the construction of a barracks and a civil hospital, and the Albert Market dates from his tenure. After
peace returned to the Kombos, O'Connor resumed his
practice of touring the upriver areas, attempting to secure a rapprochement with the riverine rulers in this
brief lull in the fighting between traditionalists and Muslims.

O'HARA, CHARLES (Colonel). An officer of the Coldstream
Guards who became, in 1765, the first Governor of the
Senegambia. He was also in command of O'Hara's Corps
comprising three companies of foot soldiers raised specifically for the defense of the territory. One company was
posted to the Gambia and was stationed at James Fort.
O'Hara devoted most of his energies to the problems of
Senegal, leaving the lieutenant-governors in the Gambia
to deal with the problems of trade, diplomacy with Gambian chiefs, and the threat of a revived France. Unfortunately, the lieutenant-governors tended to disobey orders, carry on private trade, and in general act without

restraint. In 1775, the problem of governing the Senegambia was compounded by the cruel and arbitrary actions
of Lieutenant-Governor MacNamara. Thus when O'Hara
ended his 11-year-tour, the Province was in turmoil.

OMAR OF SABAJI (Sukuta). Little is known of his life before his arrival in the Gambia except that he was a Mauritanian and had taken part in Abd-el-Kader's uprising
against the French in Algeria in 1847, where he had acquired a modicum of military training. In the Gambia, he
moved to Sabaji where in conjunction with other Marabouts
he began to organize the population disaffected by the
forced cession of their town to the British in 1853. He
was also responsible for the fiction that he had the power
to turn British bullets into water. Omar supported Fodi
Kabba in his dispute with Kombo which led directly to the
storming of the latter's town and the death of Kombo's
ruler, Suling Jatta, in June 1855. This and further disturbances at Sabaji convinced the British governor, Colonel O'Connor, to send a small military detachment to Sabaji. This force was driven out and retreated to Jesh-
wang, and after O'Connor with all of his available troops
marched to their relief, he decided to take his 260 men
and attack Sabaji directly. The people of Sabaji led by
Omar, and reinforced from other towns, trapped O'Connor's
troops. The British had to retreat, losing one fourth of
their number in killed and wounded. If Omar had pressed
his advantage, he could have bypassed O'Connor and driven
to Bathurst. With reinforcements from Barra, Kombo, and
French troops from Goree, O'Connor and the West African
regiments marched to Sabaji, and after fierce fighting, took
the town on July 15, 1855. Omar escaped and fled the
Gambia, presumably for Senegal, and thereafter was never
a factor in the Soninke-Marabout conflicts.

ORD, H. ST. GEORGE (Colonel; later Major-General). Depu-
tized in 1864 by Parliament to investigate the position of
the British West African Settlements. Although agreeing
in the main with those critics of Colonial policy who believed that these settlements were not profitable, he did
not recommend their abandonment. With special reference
to the Gambia and Freetown, he concluded that Britain had
a moral obligation to the African people who had sought
the protection of the Crown. He agreed with Governor
D'Arcy when he stated in his 1865 report that some way

should be found to extend British protection to the
troubled areas on the north bank of the Gambia River.
The select Committee of Parliament used Ord's report as
justification for a no-expansionist doctrine which became
the official British policy for two decades.

ORFEUR, CHARLES. Chief agent of the Royal African Company beginning in 1718. He had joined the company only
a few months before as a writer. His attempts to repair
Fort James and to improve the company's trade were in-
terrupted by the appearance in 1719 of pirates. They
sacked the fort, took a number of ships as prizes, and
scattered the small garrison. In 1721, Orfeur handed
over what was left of the garrison to the new governor,
Colonel Thomas Whitney. He was supplanted in command
of the trading activities by two new merchant factors.
Orfeur continued in the company's service in a subordinate position until 1723 when the death of his superiors
once more placed him in charge of the company's trading
activities. He assisted Captain Stibbs to prepare for his
upriver expedition, and commanded one of the company
ships in action in 1726 against a would-be pirate. In
mid-1727, he gave over supreme authority to Daniel Pepper who proceeded to loot the company of as much as he
could. Eventually in 1737, Orfeur was given the permanent appointment of chief agent in the Gambia, and he
endeavored to increase the company's profits despite increasing French competition and the resumption of the
wars in 1743. He was killed by some of the subjects of
the king of Barra in 1745 while on a trade mission.

ORGANIZATION FOR THE DEVELOPMENT OF THE GAMBIA
RIVER BASIN (OMVG). Established in 1978 to coordinate
the development of the Gambia River and adjacent areas
between Senegal and Gambia, its headquarters is located
at Kaolack in Senegal. Long-range plans call for the
construction of salt intrusion dams for the lower river
and a hydroelectric irrigation dam in the upper-river
reaches in Senegal. After much discussion, representatives of both states agreed to concentrate upon construct-
ing a bridge-dam at Farafeni in the Gambia to link Senegal to the Casamance via the trans-Gambian road.

OZANNE, J. H. Appointed as the first Travelling Commissioner for the north bank areas in 1893. His district

began at Suara Creek and extended past Niambantang
approximately 120 miles upriver. Like his counterpart,
F. C. Sitwell, on the south bank, he travelled the entire
area on foot, stopping at each major village to explain
their new position in the scheme of Protectorate government. Later he passed on the newest regulations which
had been decided on in Bathurst. He also adjudicated
disagreements between villages, and sat with the African
rulers when they heard civil or criminal cases. Consider-
ing the long history of disorders in his territory, Ozanne
surprisingly found little hostility or resentment. This was
due, perhaps, to the proximity of the French who were
greatly disliked by both the people and their rulers. Before being invalided home, Ozanne had firmly established
the basis of British rule in the northern segments of the
Protectorate.

-P-

PPA   see   SISAY, SHERIF

PPP   see   PEOPLE'S PROGRESSIVE PARTY

PALMER, SIR H. RICHMOND. Governor of the Gambia from
    1930 to 1933. He had previously been Lieutenant-
    Governor of Northern Nigeria and a disciple of Lord Lu-
    gard. In 1933, he issued his Political Memoranda for the
    Guidance of Commissioners..., which reflected many of
    the concepts of indirect rule as enunciated by Lugard
    and Sir Donald Cameron. He also issued a series of Or-
    dinances in 1933 designed to regularize and standardize
    government and court activities in the Protectorate. In
    the previous year he had added a second African member
    to the Legislative Council and also appointed one of the
    Commissioners of the Protectorate to the Council. This
    was the first time the Protectorate was directly repre-
    sented in the central government. In 1931, Governor
    Palmer also sponsored the formation of the advisory Ur-
    ban District Council to act as a point of contact between
    the people of the Colony and the government. This or-
    ganization later developed into the Bathurst Town Council.
    Palmer was also an accomplished Arabic scholar and his-
    torian, and in 1931 published The Carthaginian Voyage to
    West Africa in 500 B.C. together with Sultan Mohammed
    Bello's Account of the Origin of the Fulbe.

PARK, MUNGO. Scottish explorer, born in 1773 and died
in 1805 near Bussa in Nigeria. He was sponsored by the
African Association in 1795 to investigate the many rumors
connected with the Niger River, and he spent some time
studying Mandingo at Dr. Laidley's station at Karantaba
before leaving the Gambia on his first expedition. After
many hardships, he reached Segu and the Niger before
being forced to turn back. He returned to the Gambia
in September 1798 with definite proof of the existence of
the great river, and its direction of flow, and some
knowledge of the people of the western savannah. In
1805, Park, sponsored by the Colonial Office, set out from
the Gambia on his ill-fated second expedition. There
were far too many Europeans in the large entourage, and
the journey was begun during the rainy season. By the
time Bamako was reached, only Park and four companions
were healthy enough to continue. They constructed a
raft and floated down the Niger as far as Bussa where
legend claims they were drowned in the rapids. Park's
journal of the second expedition was later brought to the
coast by one of his followers, Issaco. Park's two expeditions were the tangible beginnings of the drive by Europeans to open the interior of West Africa.

PATEY, C. G. (Rear Admiral). The Administrator of the
Gambia from 1866 to 1871. He was one of the key infor-
mants for the Colonial and Foreign Offices in their attempt
to exchange the Gambia for suitable territory elsewhere in
Africa. He agreed with Sir Arthur Kennedy, his immediate supervisor, that there were few good reasons for
Britain to retain the Gambia. He reported that the cost
of maintaining the garrison was high and the bulk of the
groundnut trade was already dominated by the French.
The endemic warfare between Fodi Kabba and the Soninke
rulers of Kombo fostered his belief that little could be
done to improve the Africans adjacent to the Colony.
Patey's attitude was, without doubt, colored by the dis-
asterous cholera epidemic which struck the Colony in late
April 1869. Before the disease had run its course, over
1,100 citizens of Bathurst out of a population of 4,000
died. Patey was the Administrator during the height of
the upriver violence attendant on the rise of Alfa Molloh
and the collapse of Ma Bâ's empire.

PAUL, SIR JOHN. Governor of the Gambia from 1962 to
1965 who had the distinction of being the last British

Governor on the continent of Africa. In 1947, he joined
the Colonial Service and spent the next 15 years in
Sierra Leone as a District Officer, Provincial Officer,
and Secretary to the Cabinet. In the Gambia, he immediately established good relations with the then Chief
Minister, P. S. N'Jie, and his successor, Sir Dauda
Jawara who became the first Prime Minister. From the
first, Paul recognized that his position was transitional
and he contributed much to the framing of Gambian proposals for independence.

PEANUTS   see   GROUNDNUTS

PEOPLE'S PROGRESSIVE ALLIANCE   see   SISAY, SHERIF

PEOPLE'S PROGRESSIVE PARTY (PPP). Originally formed
by David (now Sir Dauda) Jawara, Sanjally Bojang, and
other Protectorate leaders to contest the 1960 elections.
At first it was called the Protectorate People's Party, but
the name was changed to avoid accusations of being divisive. Nevertheless, PPP support has remained strongest
in the Protectorate with its greatest support among the
Mandingo people. In the elections of 1960, the PPP won
eight seats to the House of Representatives to only six
for the United Party. This was counterbalanced, however, by the eight appointed chiefs, and when the British governor decided to appoint a Chief Minister, he selected P. S. N'Jie, the United Party leader, instead of Jawara. At the next election in 1962 for an expanded House
where the chiefs' powers had been greatly reduced, the
PPP won 18 of the contested seats. Since then the PPP
has been in control of th Gambian government, and it was
the party which negotiated independence. Despite a brief
setback on the question of a Presidential form of government in 1965, the PPP's power has continued to grow. In
the elections of 1966, the PPP won 24 of the 32 elected
seats to the House. Sir Dauda Jawara (knighted in 1966)
reintroduced his proposals for Presidential government,
and this time the people supported it at the referendum in
April 1970. The United Party during the same period was
undergoing a series of crises, and in the general elections
of 1972, the PPP won an overwhelming victory, gaining 28
seats while the United Party won only three (Colony-
based) seats.

In the ensuing years despite periodic purges in the

leadership circle by Jawara, the PPP maintained its dominance at the polls. A new party, the National Convention
Party (NCP), was formed and led by Sheriff Dibba. It
challenged the PPP in the election of 1977 for the expanded (35 member) House of Representatives. The PPP won
almost 70 percent of the popular vote and secured 28
seats. The election of 1982 produced similar results with
the PPP securing 62 percent of the vote and retaining 27
seats in the House. In both elections President Jawara
was easily elected. Over 70 percent of the electorate
chose him over his NCP opponent, Sheriff Dibba.

PETERS, LENRIE. Poet and surgeon born in Banjul in 1932.
He was educated in secondary schools in Gambia and
Freetown and graduated from Trinity College, Cambridge.
He completed medical school at University Hospital, London, in 1959 and later studied surgery at Guilford. Later,
he became a member of the Royal College of Surgeons.
Returning to Gambia, he continued the practice of medicine and became the Chief Surgeon and Director of the
Protectorate Hospital at Bansang. Leaving the civil service, he entered private practice and maintains the West-
field Clinic at Serrekunda. While still in the United Kingdom, Poems, his first collection of poetry, was published
in 1964 by Mbari Press in Ibadan. The following year he
published a semi-autobiographical novel entitled, The
Second Round. These two works brought him to the attention of literary England and he appeared on a number
of radio programs on the BBC. His reputation as one of
Africa's finest poets was enhanced by the publication of
three other works: Satellites (1967), Katchikali (1971),
and Selected Poems (1982).

PHILLIPS, MILLARD. The poultry expert from the United
States employed by Lord Trefgarne, Chairman of the
Board of the Colonial Development Corporation, to be the
field director of the Yundum egg scheme. Phillips had
been very successful with a similar project in the West
Indies. However, lack of knowledge of the Gambia and a
disinclination to accept advice from local officials led him
and his associates to project very optimistic estimates and
to downgrade the very real problems in establishing the
scheme. Grain crops met only one-quarter of the estimated production, and most of the chickens died of fowl
pest. In February 1951, the corporation decided to accept

their losses of almost one million pounds, and Phillips departed from the Gambia.

PORTENDIC. A trading station in Mauritania for those merchants who dealt in gum arabic. British theoretical rights to trade there were surrendered by a treaty with France in 1857 in exchange for the cession of Albreda on the north bank of the Gambia River.

PORTUGUESE TOWN. A section of Banjul (Bathurst) which lay west of the barracks and MacCarthy Square. The section immediately fronting on the Atlantic Ocean was, in the 19th century, a residential district for the merchants. Behind this more exclusive section was the area where most of the mulatto population of the town resided.

-Q-

QADIRIYYA. The chief Muslim tariq, or mystical brotherhood, in western Africa in the 19th century. It was the first such tariq formed to make the doctrines of Islam more intelligible to the ordinary believer, and was created by Abd al Qadir al Gilani in the 12th century.

QUIN, THOMAS F. British merchant who was described as the most substantial trader in the Gambia in the early 1860s. He had previously been in the employ of the government. Quin was one of the most vocal opponents to the two plans to exchange the Gambia for French territory. Although his fortunes in the Gambia had declined by 1875, he remained a powerful aid to the London and Manchester Chambers of Commerce in bringing pressure to bear on the government to end the negotiations with France.

QUINELLA (Kwinella). A village in Kiang. In 1863, a son of the former Soninke ruler of Baddibu attempted to overthrow Ma Bâ's powers, and having failed, recrossed the Gambia River where he and his followers regrouped themselves near Quinella. Ma Bâ's forces pursued them across the river, and there ensued one of the major pitched battles of the Soninke-Marabout Wars. Ma Bâ was defeated, his army retreated, and he was forced briefly to seek sanctuary from the Fulbe at Sumbundu. Although this

defeat was not as important a factor in the downfall of
Ma Bâ as believed by the British, it did deny him a
major foothold on the south bank and forced him to concentrate his expansionist activity northward into Saloum
and Jolof.

-R-

RAC   see   ROYAL AFRICAN CORPS

RATE PAYERS ASSOCIATION. A small Bathurst organization
formed in the late 1920s to act as a pressure group on
the British administration. The influence of the Rate
Payers Association was greatest between 1931 and 1935
when members of the newly created Urban District Council were normally chosen from its ranks. Although it continued to have a voice in Banjul affairs the Association
gradually lost its unique position after the creation of the
Bathurst Town Council in 1935.

RECAPTIVES   see   LIBERATED AFRICANS

REEVE, HENRY E. British writer and Fellow of the Royal
Geographic Society who in 1912 published a book entitled,
The Gambia. It remains a good reference work for some
aspects of African migrations and European occupation.
It is particularly valuable for the section written by Dr.
Hopkinson on animal and plant life in the Gambia at the
beginning of the century.

REFFELL, JOSEPH. The son of Thomas Reffell, born in the
early 1820s and received his formal education in Sierra
Leone. He served in the military in the Gambia, but resigned to become a river trader for a European firm. In
the 1860s, accumulated debts forced him from business.
He then became one of the chief spokesmen for the younger
generation of Liberated Africans who were openly critical
of British administration of the Colony. He was sent for
a legal education to London by Liberated African sponsors.
Although he did not complete his education, he was a regular correspondent for the African Times which articulated
the grievances of educated Africans against British rule.
In the early 1870s, Reffell became one of the most important
Gambian leaders in the struggle against Britain's proposal

to exchange the Gambia for suitable French territory elsewhere. Reffell continued even after the British decision against exchange in 1876 to be one of the most outspoken opponents of some of the oppressive aspects of British rule. In his later years he turned to agriculture and attempted to begin a cooperative farming system utilizing modern Western methods to produce tropical products for export. He died in 1886.

REFFELL, THOMAS. A Christian recaptive Igbo who in the 1820s was resettled in Bathurst from Sierra Leone. His surname was taken from the European manager of the Liberated African Department in Sierra Leone. He became a trader and was affluent enough to afford to educate his son in Sierra Leone. He served with distinction in the volunteer militia during the Barra War of 1831. In 1842, he founded the Igbo Society, a voluntary paid association open to both men and women of Igbo descent. This was the first of the Friendly Societies which became major vehicles for expressing to government the opinion of important segments of Bathurst society. Thomas Reffell died in 1849 at the age of 55.

RENDALL, GEORGE. Previously the acting Chief Justice of Sierra Leone who was appointed Lieutenant Governor of the Gambia in February 1830. He inherited the pent-up resentment of Burungai Sonko, the king of Barra, and his advisors. They felt they had been cheated by not receiving payment for the stone quarried at Dog Island, resented the cutting back on the king's subsidy, and most of all, felt the losses from custom duties after the cession of the Ceded Mile. A minor altercation between two men from Essau and the canteen operator of Fort Bullen triggered open warfare in August 1831. A motley group of soldiers, merchant sailors, and civilians decided to attack the stockaded town of Essau. They were repulsed by the townspeople with a number of casualties. The Europeans fled the scene, crossed over to Bathurst, and left Fort Bullen to the people of Essau. Governor Rendall's call for assistance was heeded by the French who sent troops and a warship. Their presence stabilized the situation near Bathurst. Burungai Sonko's forces repelled three attacks upon Essau, and by the end of the year the British had not been able to take the town. Burungai Sonko, however, decided to make peace, and in January 1832,

the Barra War can to an end. In 1834, Rendall was faced
with another threat to British supremacy in the upper
river by the actions of Chief Kemintang. A military expedition was sent against the chief's town of Dungasseen.
The British action was a fiasco and they had to abandon
three of their cannon in their retreat. Perhaps the most
telling failure of Rendall's tenure were the schemes to re-
settle Liberated Africans in the Gambia. Large numbers
were sent from Sierra Leone without proper advance planning. Some were sent to MacCarthy Island, others to the
Ceded Mile, and others were posted outside Bathurst.
With few funds and no coordination of administrative effort, there was little Rendall could do to relieve the plight
of the majority of the freed slaves, and it was left to his
successor to solve the problem of the Liberated African.
Rendall died in 1837 in Bathurst of yellow fever.

RICHARDS, SIR ARTHUR. Governor of the Gambia from
   1933 to 1936 who operated under the handicap of continued reduced revenues due to the depression. Major developments during his short tenure were the two Protectorate Ordinances which clarified the major Protectorate
   Ordinance of 1933 and established a new yard tax rate.

RIP   see   BADDIBU

ROWE, SIR SAMUEL. Army surgeon and Colonial Office administrator posted to West Africa in 1862. He served in
   the Ashanti War of 1873-74 and was then appointed Administrator of the Gambia where he served from 1875 to
   1876. He was Governor of the West African Settlements
   (Sierra Leone and the Gambia) from 1876 to 1881, Governor
   of Lagos and the Gold Coast from 1881 to 1884, and again
   Governor of the West African Settlements from 1884 to
   1888. Rowe was a staunch imperialist who believed that
   both Britain and the Africans would prosper by extension
   of British rule into the hinterland. He opposed the schemes
   for exchanging the Gambia, and was an implacable foe of
   the Colonial Office policy of surrendering to French demands in the Mellacourie, Porto Novo, and the Gambian
   interior. It was Rowe who planned the expedition of Administrator Gouldsbury into the upper Gambia.

ROYAL ADVENTURES OF ENGLAND TRADING INTO AFRICA.
   A company chartered by Charles II to trade in West Africa.

The glowing reports made by Prince Rupert were fundamental to the establishment of this company. Despite
Royal support, particularly from James, Duke of York,
the Adventurers did not find that trade was very profitable. The major reasons for lack of profits were trade
losses incurred in the second Dutch war. In 1668, the
Royal Adventurers sublet their monopoly to another trading company called the Gambia Adventurers, and in 1684
relinquished it completely to the Royal African Company.

ROYAL AFRICAN COMPANY. An English chartered company
which assumed a monopoly of trade in West Africa in 1684.
Although the main area of company concern was the Gold
Coast, the company did have a considerable investment in
the Gambia. The main base in the Gambia as with previous trading companies was James Island. The chief factor
of the company was in command of a small number of soldiers and an even smaller civilian staff. In addition to
James Island, the company maintained other stations along
the river. The number of these outstations varied, but
there normally was trading activity on MacCarthy Island,
near Barrakunda Falls, at Bintang, Banyon Point, and
Juffure. At best, the profit levels were low since there
were few natural products in the area and the Gambia
never was an important slave trading entrepôt. Health
conditions for servants of the company were so poor that
the stations were always understaffed and there was a
high turnover of personnel. Far more disastrous to
the company were the long series of European wars which
pitted France against England. Local conflict with the
French dated from 1681 when they established a trading
post at Albreda on the north bank opposite James Island.
A French naval squadron forced abandonment of James
Island in 1693, and it was not reoccupied until 1698. In
this year also, Parliament declared the West African trade
open to all English merchants. The Royal African Company was still charged with the upkeep of the trade forts
and could level a 10 percent duty on all goods imported
and exported to West Africa. During the War of Spanish
Succession, James Island was plundered by the French in
1704 and 1708. Only the exhaustion of the rival French
company saved the company from further depredations.
The fort on James Island was rebuilt and reoccupied in
1717, but pirates sacked the island, and within four years
it was necessary to send a new expedition to restore the

fortunes of the company. An attempt at sending European colonists in the 1720s proved a ghastly failure. The
period between 1730 to 1740 was the most prosperous in
the long history of the company. There was peace in
Europe, the slave and gum trade was profitable, and the
company received a subsidy from Parliament. The War of
Austrian Succession ended this. Although the English
destroyed Albreda, the war disturbed trade, and sickness and death forced the closing of the outstations and
near abandonment of James Fort. In 1747, Parliament
cancelled the Parliamentary subsidy, and in 1752, the
Royal African Company was finally dissolved by Parliamentary action.

ROYAL AFRICAN CORPS (RAC). Formed in 1765 and composed largely of men drawn from the convict hulks in
England or military offenders from other regiments, it
nevertheless played an important role in the suppression
of the slave trade since men of the Corps served not only
on land, but also on ships of the West African Patrol.
At first it comprised three companies of foot soldiers and
was called O'Hara's Corps, named for the first governor
of the Senegambia. Men of the Royal African Corps, under the command of Captain Alexander Grant, were responsible for occupying first James Island and then St.
Mary's Island in 1816, and they later constructed the
barracks and other public buildings in Bathurst. Disease took a frightening toll of the European common soldiers. Between May 1825 and July 1827, 276 of a total
of 399 European soldiers landed at Bathurst died. After
1827, all European soldiers in the Gambia were replaced
by Africans or West Indian troops.

RUPERT, PRINCE OF THE PALATINATE. A nephew of King
Charles I of England, and during the Civil War, one of
the king's better generals. He accompanied the future
Charles II into exile and took every opportunity of strik-
ing at the English Commonwealth government. One such
venture concerned the Gambia when Rupert, preying on
English commerce, arrived at the estuary of the Gambia
River in February 1652. Learning of the presence of
three ships of the Commonwealth which had accompanied
John Blake on his trading expedition, Rupert sailed upriver to St. Andrew's Island where he received assistance
from the Courlander commander. He attacked Blake's ships

and captured them, and then sailed from the river northward to Cape Verde where one of his landing parties was
captured by the Wolof near Rufisque. Rupert freed his
men, but was wounded by an arrow. He then left West
Africa for the West Indies. While in the Gambia, Rupert
came to believe the reports of huge gold deposits in the
hinterland. Later after the restoration, this story played
an important role in the formation of the Royal Adventurers. Prince Rupert was one of the main sponsors and in-
vestors in that company.

-S-

SARDU, BAKARI. Ruler of Bondu in the 1860s and 1870s.
He had received a French education, was awarded the
Legion of Honor, and throughout his career was very
careful not to alienate the French. He became vitally
involved with the upper river areas of the Gambia in
checking the ambitions of his fellow rulers, and also for
economic gain. In 1866, he led a major invasion through
Wuli that briefly threatened MacCarthy Island. This operation forced the British to abandon their policy of retreat and to send troops to the island. In the 1870s,
Bakari Sardu formed an unofficial Fulbe coalition with
Alfa Ibrahima of Futa Jallon and Alfa Molloh. In that
period his forces made almost annual raids into the Gambia. Sardu, depending on the circumstances, would ally
himself either with Soninke or Marabout factions in the
Gambia.

SARR, SAMUEL JOHNSON. A businessman and diplomat, he
was born in Bathurst in 1921 and was educated at Methodist Elementary School and Methodist Boys High School
(1938-40). Employed by British Overseas Airways (1942-
47), West African Airways (1947-57), becoming senior station officer at Jos, Nigeria, before assuming the position
as station manager in Bathurst. He became a member of
the Gambia Oilseeds Marketing Board in 1958 and the same
year he was awarded membership in the British Empire
(MBE). He became a member of the Gambia Tourist Board
and President of the Gambia Tourist Association in 1967,
a position he held until 1971 when he was appointed Gambian High Commissioner to Senegal with Plenipotentiary
powers to Guinea, Liberia, Sierra Leone, Mali, Mauritania,

and Guinea Bissau. In 1974 he was designated Gambian
High Commissioner to Nigeria, a post he held for nine
years becoming dean of the Diplomatic Corps in that state.
In 1983 he was accredited to the United Kingdom as Gambia's High Commissioner with concurrent powers as Ambassador Plenipotentiary to Austria, Denmark, Norway,
Sweden, Switzerland, and the Vatican.

SATIYO-TIYO. Figuratively means owner of the land. This
person was the village head, also called at times an alkali.
He was normally the eldest member of a lineage which was
recognized as having titular rights to their office.

SEAGRAM, HENRY F. First Governor of the independent
Colony of the Gambia in 1843, who died of the fever only
a few months after assuming the office and before he
could significantly effect any changes in the Colony.

SEITANE. Wolof term for the devil who can make people
mad, can change a normal child into one who is abnormal
or deformed, and can adversely affect the outcome of
normal decision making.

SELECT COMMITTEE OF PARLIAMENT (1842). Created primarily as a response to the activities of George MacLean,
the company administrator in the Gold Coast. The Committee called into question the methodology of British
government in all the West African areas. As a result
of its recommendations, the Crown assumed direct control
over the Gold Coast and the decision was taken to allow
each British territory to have its own administration without reference to a governor-in-chief. The first governor
of the Gambia under these new regulations was Captain
H. F. Seagram.

SELECT COMMITTEE OF PARLIAMENT (1865). Created because of Parliamentary pressure to reduce the cost of ad-
ministering the Empire. The Committee based its recommendations largely upon the report of Colonel H. St.
George Ord. It enunciated the doctrine of no territorial
expansion in Africa which remained the dominant Colonial
philosophy for over twenty years. The Colonial Office,
following the report of the Committee, ordered the abandonment of MacCarthy Island. British presence in the
vicinity of MacCarthy Island was left to a factor who was

also a trader in the upper river areas. He had no official
authority and had to operate without benefit of British
troops. More important for the Gambia, the Select Committee recommended that all British West African possessions be placed once again under the direct control of a
governor-in-chief, resident in Freetown. This was ef-
fected by 1866. In 1874, Lagos and the Gold Coast were
removed from such control, but the Gambia remained under such control until 1888. The chief executive officer
resident in the Gambia was called an Administrator.

SENEGAL, CLOSER ASSOCIATION WITH see CLOSER
    ASSOCIATION WITH SENEGAL

SENEGAL COMPANY. A short-lived, but important commer-
    cial company established by the French in 1672 as a suc-
    cessor to Colbert's grandiose West Indies Company. In
    1677, a French fleet captured Goree from the Dutch, and
    this became the main base of operations for the company.
    In the next few years, the company, in conjunction with
    French naval vessels, harassed the shipping of the Royal
    African Company and attempted to supplant the English
    on the Gambia River. Factors were established at a num-
    ber of locales south of Cape Verde, a punitive expedition
    was mounted against Saloum, and in 1681, the first trad-
    ing station at Albreda was built opposite James Island.
    The outbreak of war in 1689 reversed the fortunes of the
    company, and they gave up their monopoly first to the
    Guinea Company, and finally in 1696 to the Royal Senegal
    Company.

SENEGAMBIA, PROVINCE OF. During the Seven Years War,
    the British occupied and garrisoned the Senegambia. At
    the conclusion of the war, administration of the area was
    vested in a Committee of Merchants. Revived French ac-
    tivity and the weakness of the company caused a rever-
    sion of the territory to the Crown in 1765 under the name
    Province of the Senegambia. The government system was
    based on that of an American colony with a Governor,
    Council, and Chief Justice. The first governor was Colo-
    nel O'Hara who also commanded three companies of troops
    known as O'Hara's Corps, but later renamed the Royal
    African Corps. O'Hara's 11-year tenure of office was
    marked by continued difficulties with French traders on
    the Gambia River and even more vexing problems of con-

trolling the actions of the lieutenant-governors and their
troops at James Island. Matthias MacNamara, who had
exercised almost independent command in the Gambia,
succeeded O'Hara as governor and almost immediately became embroiled with Captain Wall, his lieutenant in the
Gambia. This struggle, which culminated in MacNamara's
removal, weakened the entire government of the province
at a time when the French had decided to aid the American Revolution. MacNamara's successor, Governor Clarke,
died in August 1778, and only an ensign was in command
at St. Louis in January 1779 when a French fleet appeared
and seized the station. The following month, the French
forced the surrender of James Island and razed the fort
there. Later in the year, a British squadron occupied
Goree, but found James Fort to be in no condition to be
assigned as a garrison and no further attempts were made
to occupy any territory in the Gambia during the war.
The Treaty of Versailles in 1783 returned all of the Province of Senegambia to France with the exception of the
Gambia River and James Island, which were retained by
the British. See also CONFEDERATION OF SENEGAMBIA.

SERAHULI. Inhabitants of part of the area which once was
    the ancient kingdom of Wuli. Today they form the largest
    population block in the extreme upper river areas of the
    Gambia. They are mixtures of Mandingo, Berber, and
    Fulbe. They are primarily farmers, handicapped more
    than other peoples of the Gambia because of the poorness
    of the soil. The Serahuli have in the past suffered great-
    ly from food shortages, and the hungry season was an
    ever-present factor in their lives until the close of the
    1950s. In the course of the Soninke-Marabout Wars of
    the 19th century, many Serahuli became mercenaries will-
    ing to serve in the armies of either side.

SERER. According to their traditions, the Serer were an
    agricultural people who resided in Futa Toro when a ser-
    ies of invasions by the Fulbe drove them southward.
    Long association with Wolof, Fulbe, and Mandingo has
    produced a complex racial admixture of the Serer. The
    Serer speak a language classified by Joseph H. Greenberg
    as a part of the northern sub-group of the Niger-
    Kordofanian family and is closely akin to Paolar, the
    language of the Fulbe and Tucolor. The bulk of the
    nearly one-half million Serer lives in the Sine and Saloum

area of Senegal. Two neighboring peoples, the Serer
N'Dieghem and the Niominka, are considered branches of
the Serer although they speak different dialects and had
more simplified political systems. The main group of
Serer were referred to by early European travellers as
"Barbesins" meaning people of the Bur Sine. After the
mid-19th century the two Serer kingdoms occupied very
strategic locations, blocking southward expansion of the
French and also the ambitions of Ma Bâ of Baddibu. In
both states, peanut cultivation became very important for
the Serer peasants as well as the French merchants. The
Serer had a complex social and political organization in
each of their two kingdoms. The burs or kings, chosen
from the guelowar (matrilineage of the Mandingo founders
of their states), secure in the prosperity of their farming
villages, could command very large armies (tyeddos). The
Bur Sine and the Sine tyeddo were responsible for the
defeat and death of Ma Bâ in 1867 which ended all chances
for a unified Muslim polity in the Senegambia. The Serer
population in the Gambia is very small, numbering under
10,000 persons.

SEYFU (pl.: Seyfolu). Mandingo word meaning chief or
ruler. This was the title used by the British for all the
35 chiefs of the modern Protectorate.

SILLA, FODI see TOURE, FODI SILLA

SIMOTTO MORO. A Torodo Fulbe, a Muslim teacher, and a
resident in Fuladu in the 1860s who had gathered around
him a group of disciples. He appeared to Alfa and Musa
Molloh as a threat to their complete control of Fuladu.
Before they could act against him, he moved with his
followers across the Gambia River to Wuli and there established the heavily fortified town of Toubacouta which
in a short time became a center for trade and learning in
the upper river area. Disaffected Fulbe from Fuladu reinforced Simotto Moro's power, and until his death in 1881,
Toubacouta was safe from attack from Fuladu.

SINGHATEH, ALHAJI FARIMANG MAMADI. The first Gambian-
born Governor of the Gambia, succeeding Sir John Paul in
December 1965. He was born at Georgetown in 1912 of an
old Mandingo family, but was later adopted by a British District Officer who helped educate him at local primary schools

and at Armitage. Beginning in 1935, he was associated
with the Medical Department. He qualified as a pharmacist
in 1950, and after retiring from the Civil Service in 1963,
operated his own pharmacy at Farafenni. He had been
Chairman of the Protectorate Welfare Societies before becoming associated with the People's Progressive Party
which he supported although he was never politically active. He was appointed a member of the Public Service
Commission in 1964, the highest position held before his
appointment as Governor.

SISAY, SHERIF. Politician, born in 1935 at Kudag in the
Protectorate, one of the children of Sekuba Sisay, chief
of Niamina District from 1927 to 1952. He was educated
in Koranic schools and spent eight years at the Secondary
School in Georgetown. In 1957, he became a clerk in the
Education Department, and was a founder member of the
People's Progressive Party. He became its first Secretary-
General in 1959, a post he held until he broke with the
party in 1968. In the 1960 elections, he was one of the
nine PPP members elected to the House of Assembly, and
he was appointed a minister without portfolio in the Executive Council. In March 1961, with the other PPP members,
he resigned because the governor appointed P. S. N'Jie
of the United Party as Chief Minister. However, the 1962
elections gave the PPP a definitive majority, and Sisay
became the Finance Minister and was normally recognized
as the number two man in the government. As Finance
Minister, Sisay framed a series of budgets which reflected
Gambia's modest economic position, but which did allow
for needed development and growth. In September 1968,
after some disagreement with the other leaders of the PPP,
Sisay and three other young politicians were expelled from
the party. In October, he was instrumental in forming a
new political vehicle, the People's Progressive Alliance
(PPA), which joined the United Party in opposition. The
PPA vehemently opposed the government's proposal for a
Republic until just before the April 1970 plebiscite when
the party leaders reversed themselves. The fortunes of
the PPA declined rapidly after 1970 and Sisay rejoined
the PPP serving as a member of Parliament until President
Jawara called upon him to rejoin his ministry. In late
1982 he replaced Saiku Sabally as Minister of Trade and
Finance.

SITWELL, F. C. Appointed the first Travelling Commissioner
for the south bank areas of the Protectorate in January
1893. He was thus the first permanent British official in
all the troubled areas from Kombo to Niamina. With his
partner, J. H. Ozanne, the north bank Commissioner, he
represented the Crown to the peoples of approximately
150 miles of riverine territory. Since he had no military
or police escort, he had to be very diplomatic in informing
the chiefs and the people of their new status and of the
laws and ordinances of the Colony which applied to them.
He also tried to act as a neutral judge in any dispute
which arose between villages or chiefdoms. Although more
Travelling Commissioners were appointed in the late 1890s,
their tasks were made even more difficult by the enact-
ment of the Protectorate Ordinance of 1894, the Yard Tax
Ordinance, and the Public Lands Ordinance of 1897. In
1899, a long-standing dispute over rice land flared between the Soninkes of Jataba and the Marabouts of Sankandi. Sitwell adjudicated the matter and decided in
favor of Jataba. The Marabouts of Sankandi, mostly followers of Fodi Kabba, refused to abide by the decision.
Sitwell, accompanied by his replacement, F. E. Silva, 11
African constables, and Mansa Koto, the chief of Battelling, proceeded to Sankandi in early 1900 to enforce the
land decision. After a brief discussion, Sitwell's group
proceeded to the center of the town, an argument developed, and some of the Marabouts opened fire. Sitwell,
Silva, Mansa Koto, and six constables were killed. The
violence done to Sitwell's party convinced both the British and French governments that the interior regions had
to be pacified and led to the joint military expedition of
1901.

SLAVE TRADE. Slavery was an indigenous institution among
all the peoples of the Gambia. It was converted by the
Atlantic slave trade into a mutually profitable business
for both Africans and Europeans. The Portuguese in
their earliest voyages captured slaves, but slave-trading
did not become important until the 16th century with the
development of plantation economies in the Western Hemi-
sphere. The earliest English and French traders to the
Gambia were more concerned with gum, gold, and ivory,
and Richard Jobson in the 17th century indignantly refused to trade in slaves. However, by the 18th century,
traffic in slaves was the most important business of the

Royal African Company. Even then the Gambia was not
considered a good recruiting area, most of the trading
being done along the Gold Coast, Dahomey, and western
Nigeria. There are no reliable figures for the numbers
transported from the Gambia. In peak years perhaps as
many as 2,000 were sold, but according to Moore, the
average during the first quarter of the 18th century was
1,000 per year. British abolition in 1807 dealt a major
blow to the slave trade, but slave ships continued to operate in the Gambia region for decades afterward, and individual rulers such as Fodi Kabba continued to pursue
the practice throughout the 19th century. One of the
major reasons for the occupation of Bathurst (Banjul)
was the British desire to block the trade in slaves from
the Gambia River.

SMALL, EDWARD. Journalist, labor leader, and politician,
educated in Bathurst. In 1922 he founded the earliest
influential Gambian newspaper, The Gambia Outlook, first
published in Dakar because Small had no press. He was
one of the first Gambians to think in nationalist and Pan-
African terms and with Casley-Hayford of the Gold Coast
was one of the organizers of the West African National
Congress movement in the 1920s. In 1929, he founded
the Bathurst-based Gambia Labor Union, and in that year
led a successful strike of artisans and river craft workers. The union continued to be weak, primarily because
of government attitudes, but it remained, for over two
decades, the only attempt to organize Gambian workers.
Small's activities were mainly responsible for the important
Gambia Trade Union Ordinance of 1932. He was nominated
for a seat on the general executive council of the International Confederation of Free Trade Unions, and held that
position from 1945 until his death in January 1957. In
the early 1930s, Small helped organize, and became the
Chairman of, the Rate Payers' Association which always
returned candidates to the Urban District Council. He
was nominated to the Legislative Council in the early
1940s and won election to a seat on that body in 1947.
In 1951, he was defeated for reelection by I. M. Garba-
Jahumpa and J. C. Faye.

SOLDIER TOWN. A section of Banjul (Bathurst) lying south-
east of Albion Place. This was the area where most of the
discharged soldiers resided in the early 19th century.

SONINKE. A term which literally means giver of libations.
In the upper Senegal River area, it is a name given to a
people who are also called Sarakolle by the French and
Serahuli by the British. It is also a term applied to the
ancient rulers of the West African empire of Ghana. In
the Gambia in the 19th century, this term applied to the
traditionalist faction in the religious conflicts of the 19th
century. To the Marabouts, the term had similar pejora-
tive connotations as that of the term Kaffir to South Africans.

SONINKE-MARABOUT WARS. A series of conflicts which began in the mid-1850s between Islamic converts and those
Gambian leaders representing traditional political and religious interests. At one time or another, these conflicts
affected all of the riverine areas of the Gambia. The
most significant long range effects of the wars was the
destruction of most of the older Mandingo polities and the
creation of new states, and the conversion of most of the
Gambian population to Islam. The wars peaked in the two
decades after 1860 with the conquests of Ma Bâ, Alfa Molloh, and Fodi Kabba. They did not officially end until
the death of Fodi Kabba in 1901. (For further details of
the Soninke-Marabout Wars, see MOLLOH, ALFA; MOLLOH,
MUSA; BÂ; KABBA; SILLA; SONKO; D'ARCY; O'CONNOR.)

SONKO, BURUNGAI. Became the ruler of Barra in 1823, and
three years later signed a convention with Alexander Grant
giving the British control of the Ceded Mile, upon which
they constructed Fort Bullen. During the next five years,
the king came to regret the loss of his customs revenues,
and pressured by under chiefs, adopted an anti-British
attitude. Because of actions against Bathurst traders in
Niumi, the British suspended their annual payments to
him. His attitude and the foolishness of European and
African traders in Bathurst led to the Barra War. A
slight incident in August 1831, between two intoxicated
subjects of the king and the canteen keeper at Fort Bullen, led to an attempt to take Essau by a motley assort-
ment of Bathurst citizens and soldiers. They were repulsed with severe losses, and the British abandoned Barra to the king. Governor Rendell, fearing collaboration
between Sonko and the king of Kombo, pleaded for assistance from the French at Goree. With French help, a
further futile attempt was made to take Essau. Later,

even after reinforcements had arrived from Sierra Leone,
the British were unable to capture the town. The king's
subjects had, nevertheless, suffered heavily from the war,
and Burungai Sonko made peace in January 1932, recon-
firming the Ceded Mile Treaty.

SOUTHORN, LADY BELLA. Sister of Leonard Woolf and
sister-in-law of the novelist Virginia Woolf, and wife of
Governor Sir Wilfred Thomas Southorn. Lady Southorn
was also an author of considerable distinction who wrote
many articles concerning the Gambia. In 1952 she published an interesting, informative extended essay on Gambian history, society, and politics entitled, The Gambia:
The Story of the Groundnut Colony.

SOUTHORN, SIR WILFRED THOMAS. Governor of the Gambia
from 1936 to 1942. Any plans he had for major improvements either for the Colony or the Protectorate had to be
framed within the context of revenues expected from an
economically non-viable area still recovering from the
depression. After 1939, the economy of the Gambia improved substantially as the Gambia became an important
staging area during World War II. The period between
1940 and 1942 was particularly tense because the Gambia
was surrounded on three sides by Senegal whose government was controlled by Vichy France.

SPEER, FRANCIS. A minor merchant in the Gambia who had
come to the territory as a doctor in 1876. In 1879, he
had lengthy conversations with the French chargé d'affaires
in London concerning reopening discussions on an exchange
of the Gambia. The French were led to believe that Speer
was a spokesman for the Bathurst merchants, and he reported that they were only concerned with making a profit from their investments. Within a short time, Speer's
real position became known and the French did not at that
time officially present any proposals to the British Government.

STIBBS, BARTHOLOMEW (Captain). Sent to the Gambia by
the Royal African Company in 1723 with the specific purpose of searching for the legendary upriver gold mines
mentioned by Prince Rupert and Vermuyden. He reached
Barrakunda Falls in February 1724, and proceeded approximately sixty miles above them before turning back. Stibbs

reported that he found no minerals and considered Vermuyden's report to be a myth. His negative report dis-
couraged the company from further exploration. Captain
Stibbs' expedition has been recorded in Frances Moore's
Travels into the Inland Parts of Africa. Stibbs later returned to the Gambia as a merchant of the company and
had a role in the affairs of 1729-30 when some of the disaffected Europeans on James Island threatened to revolt
and blow up the fort.

STIEL, OTTO. The third chief agent of Courland in the
Gambia. He was appointed in 1653 and spent six years
in the area trying to improve trade and diplomatic relations with the mid-river Gambians. However, his successes were compromised by European disturbances.
Courlander ships were seized by both the Dutch and the
English in their commercial war. The Dutch at Goree did
not wish trade competition in the Senegambia from inter-
lopers, and twice captured the fort on St. Andrew's Island and Stiel was made prisoner each time. His release
was forced the first time by the actions of a French pri-
vateer in Swedish employ and the second time by forces
loyal to the king of Barra. The capture of James, Duke
of Courland, by the Swedes following a dynastic dispute,
and the subsequent agreement reached by Courland and
England in 1664 which ceded St. Andrew's Island, undercut all of Stiel's work in the Gambia.

STONE CIRCLES. Megaliths still of unknown origin found in
western Africa from the southern Sahara in the north to
Guinea-Bissau in the south. Most of them are located in
Senegal. All except two of the circles in the Gambia are
on the north bank. They are composed of between 10
and 20 standing laterite stones which vary in height from
two to eight feet. These stones are arranged in circles
between 10 and 20 feet in diameter. In some locales there
is a complex of circles. Wassu has 11 circles and Ker-
Batch has nine. The stones were cut from neighboring
hillsides and some of the larger stones weigh as much as
10 tons. Their transportation to the circle sites involved
a considerable labor force and complex organization. Professional and amateur excavations indicate that the area
within some of the circles was used as a burial place.
Some skeletons and many artifacts have been uncovered.
Present-day Gambians in the vicinity of the circles have

no clear notion of their origin or use. The best specula-
tion of professionals is that the circles belong to the pre-
Islamic period, perhaps as early as the 13th century, and
were constructed by either the Jola, Serer, or Mandingo
people.

STRANGE FARMERS. Landless men who migrated seasonally
to the Gambia to help with planting and harvesting crops.
During the Soninke-Marabout Wars, they served the additional function of mercenaries. During the 20th century,
the strange farmers would make their own contracts with
village headmen and be assigned to work for specific farmers in a village. They were assigned portions of land to
work for themselves in their free time, and would also
normally be required to grow a part of the additional food
supply needed for their sustenance. The pressure upon
available food supplies in the Gambia after 1945 caused
the Colonial government and the chiefs to take steps to
limit the immigration of these foreigners into the Gambia.

SUMA. Among the Mandingo kingdoms, certain village leaders had more authority over a larger area of land than
other alkali. These lineage leaders were called suma. In
Baddibu, Jarra, Niumi, Kiang, and Kombo, the kingship
rotated between certain lineages with the suma of a particular lineage becoming the mansa or king.

SUMAKUNDA. The lineage in direct line of succession to the
kingship in Mandingo kingdoms.

-T-

TALL, AL HAJJ UMAR. The khalifa of the Tijaniyya tariq
in the western Sudan, born about 1790, educated in the
Futa Toro, and later travelled widely including a five-
year pilgrimage to Mecca. In North Africa, he came under the influence of Ahamd al Tijani whose teachings
stressed the special place in paradise reserved by Allah
for the faithful. Umar later lived in Hausaland where he
married one of the daughters of Sultan Bello of Sokoto.
In 1838, he left Hausaland and established a religious and
military base at Dinguiray. By 1852 his following was
large enough to declare a jihad against the Bambara, and
he conquered Kaarta. In the decade after 1852, Umar's

followers conquered Segu and Macina, and gained control
of the upper Senegal River area. In 1863, Umar's prestige was at its zenith with the capture of Timbuktu. In
the same year he was killed suppressing a revolt in Macina. He bequeathed a huge but heterogeneous empire
to his son, Ahmadu. Umar's teaching and example of
conquering the territories of unbelievers had a great influence upon Muslim teachers in the Senegambia. Ma Bâ
and Alfa Molloh both had direct connections with the Tijaniyya movement.

TANCROWALL. A Portuguese settlement sited in the locale
of the modern village of Tankular. There was a church
with priest in residence there as late as 1730. The Royal
African Company briefly had a factory at Tancrowall in
the 1730s.

TARIQ. A subdivision of Islam comprising those individuals
who subscribe to a common philosophy and ritual. The
two most celebrated tariq brotherhoods in West Africa
were the Qadiriyya, reflecting the attitudes of the more
conservative Muslim teachers, and the Tijaniyya, founded
in 1781, which demanded of its followers more puritanical
personal and social attitudes. The Tijaniyya was particularly important in the Senegambia during the latter 19th
century in destroying the power of the older "pagan"
dynasties.

THOMAS, G. J. (Sergeant). Policeman and administrator.
He was sent by Administrator Carter to Baddibu in 1885
to attempt to bring an end to the fighting between the
forces of Mamadou N'Dare, Saër Maty, and Biram Cisse.
In 1889, he was appointed manager of British Kombo and
later took part in the Tonataba expedition of 1892 and that
of Sankandi in 1901. He retired in 1903 and died in 1935.

THOMPSON, GEORGE. Explorer and servant of the British
Guinea Company sent to the Gambia River in 1618. Despite the massacre of a number of his men by the Portuguese, Thompson was optimistic that contact with the upper river would produce a wealth of gold. In 1619, with
a few companions, he reached Tenda above Barrakunda
Falls. Thompson wanted to proceed further into the
hinterland, but his associates refused. In the ensuing
quarrel, Thompson was killed. All of his discoveries and

observations perished with him since he had committed
nothing to writing. It was left for Richard Jobson the
following year to retrace Thompson's journey and record
his findings for his superiors in London.

TIJANIYYA. A Muslim tariq or voluntary brotherhood,
founded in the late 18th century in North Africa. It
was more democratic than other tariqs, imposed fewer
obligations on the believers, and was simple to under-
stand. It was also much more puritanical and the members came to view themselves as an elite group within
Islam. The most important of the Tijaniyya leaders in
the Senegambia was Al Hajj Umar, the khalifa of the
western Sudan who in the decade after 1850 created a
large, heterogenous empire which stretched from the
middle Senegal River are past Timbuktu. Tijaniyya teachers were at the forefront of the Soninke-Marabout disturbances in the Gambia. Ma Bâ of Baddibu and Alfa Molloh
both had Tijaniyya connections.

TOMANI. One of the nine Mandingo kingdoms located along
the south bank of the Gambia River in the early 19th
century. It stretched from a point opposite Sami Creek
to Tubakuta. The Mandingo ruling dynasty was overthrown by Alfa Molloh in the late 1860s and was incorporated into the new state of Fuladu. In the 20th-century
reorganization of Gambian chiefdoms, the area which was
Tomani became the District of Fuladu East.

TORODBE FULBE. A dialect group of the Fulbe related to
their occupation as scholars. Although fewer in number
than the other Fulbe groups, they had profound impact
on the history of the upper Gambia since most Torodbe
were Muslims and their inherent position gave them the
opportunity to influence other Muslim groups at the beginning of the Soninke-Marabout conflicts.

TOURE, FODI SILLA. Emerged in the early 1870s as the
leader of the Marabout forces in Kombo. By 1874, the
Marabouts had taken Brikama and most of the major towns
in eastern Kombo. Many Soninke fled to safety in British
Kombo and some, using this as a place of sanctuary,
raided into Marabout territory. Because of the inherent
danger in this to British Kombo, Sir Cornelius Kortright,
the Administrator, in 1874 concluded a treaty with Fodi

Silla which created a neutral zone between Yundum and
British territory. The arrangements were violated by
both Soninke and Marabouts, and in the following year,
Fodi Silla's forces were everywhere victorious over those
of the king of Kombo, Tomani Bojang. The king was
forced to retreat to Lamin, a town within a few yards of
the border of British Kombo. The rainy season prevented
open warfare between Fodi Silla and the British. Tomani
Bojang, receiving no direct assistance from the British,
capitulated in September 1875, and agreed to become a
Muslim. Fodi Silla then allowed him and his people to
continue to live in Kombo. Fodi Silla then became the
dominant factor in all of the Kombo, having established
good relations with his neighbor and fellow Marabout
leader, Fodi Kabba. Except for his slave raiding activities, he caused the British administrators little trouble
until the joint Anglo-French Boundary Commission arrived
in his territory in 1891. Understandably outraged at the
implications of the Franco-British Convention of 1889,
both Fodi Silla and Fodi Kabba attempted to interfere with
the work of the Commissioners. Subsequently three gunboats were stationed near the areas where the Commission
was working. This show of force and the military actions
taken against Fodi Kabba in Foni, Kiang, and Jarra,
caused Fodi Silla to remain relatively quiet in 1892. The
British recognized him as chief of Western Kombo and paid
him a stipend. Minor problems related to Bathurst based
traders in his territory and his attitude toward the slave
trade caused the British in February 1894 to mount a two-
pronged offensive against him. After initial failures, the
British West Indian troops took Gunjur and forced Fodi
Silla to flee to Foni. The Jola leaders there refused him
sanctuary, and he and his followers retreated to the Casamance. There his followers were disarmed by the French.
Fodi Silla was deported to St. Louis and later died in exile.

TREGASKIS, THE REV. BENJAMIN. Superintendent of the
Wesleyan Mission in Sierra Leone and the Gambia from
1864 to 1870. He held a district meeting in early 1871
in Bathurst which passed a resolution condemning any
transfer of the Gambia to France, thus joining the Wesleyans with the bulk of the business community in opposition to Colonial Office policy.

TUBAB. Mandinka term for a European or white person; in

general use throughout the Senegambia. By extension it
can also refer to anyone who dresses or lives in the
European manner.

TYEDDO. Warriors in service to a Wolof or Serer king or
chief who were selected from the jam or slave class. They
were also known as slaves of the crown.

-U-

UNITED PARTY (UP). Formed in October 1951, after the
failure of Pierre Sarr N'Jie, a Bathurst barrister, to be
elected to the Legislative Council. The United Party was
a party which from the first showed great strength in the
Colony area, particularly among the Wolof. The party
was successful in returning N'Jie to the Legislative Council at the head of the poll in the elections of 1954. The
following year, N'Jie disagreed with the governor and resigned from the government. The UP thus escaped the
stigma attached to the older parties of being tools of the
British administration. In the election of 1960 when the
franchise was extended to the Protectorate, the UP elected
six members to the House of Representatives. The newly
created People's Progressive Party proved to have more
popular support in the Protectorate, returning eight members. However, in 1961, the British governor turned to
N'Jie to be the new Chief Minister, and until the elections
of 1962, the UP, in liaison with the Protectorate chiefs,
controlled the government. The new Constitution under
which the 1962 elections were held reduced the chiefs'
power to only a nominal degree, and the UP won only 13
seats to the House of Representatives as compared to 18
for the PPP. The influence of the UP after Gambian independence in 1965 continued to decline. In the elections
of 1966, despite a coalition with the Congress Party, the
UP could win only Colony seats while the PPP won 24
Protectorate seats. The UP became deeply divided over
policy, and in May 1970, P. S. N'Jie was removed as the
party leader and replaced by his brother, Ebrimah Dowda
N'Jie. On the death of E. D., the party's councils once
more selected P. S. as leader. The lowest point in the
fortunes of the UP came when the House of Representatives removed P. S. N'Jie from its roster because of non-
attendance. From this time forward the United Party

ceased to be influential in Gambian politics. In the 1972
elections only two members of the party were elected to
the House. The newly formed National Convention Party
(NCP) became the major voice of the opposition to the PPP.

USIDIMARE, ANTONIOTTO. A Genoese sea captain in the
employ of the Portuguese. In 1455, he was commissioned
by Prince Henry to explore the coastline south of Cape
Verde. In early 1456, he was joined off Cape Verde by
the ship commanded by Alvise da Cadamosto. The two
explorers led the first European explorations of the estuary of the Gambia River. In a second exploration, they
were escorted inland approximately 60 miles, and spent
over two weeks conversing and trading with Gambian rulers. Leaving the Gambia River, Usidimare proceeded to
sail southward as far south as Cape Mesurado before returning to Portugal.

USTICK, STEPHEN. A factor assigned to James Island by
Major Robert Holmes in 1661. Left in command of 29 men
in the fort, he twice resisted the attempts of Peter Justobaque, chief factor of the Dutch West Indies Company, to
seize all the recently acquired British strongholds in the
Gambia.

-V-

VALENTINE, LOUIS FRANCIS. A civil servant and High
Commissioner to Britain, born in 1908 in Bathurst. He
was educated at Methodist Boys High School and later
Fourah Bay College where he received a B.A. in 1930.
Three years later he entered the Civil Service and be-
came a senior administrator in 1949, serving in a number
of departments. In 1960, he was appointed Postmaster-
General and two years later became the first Gambian
Chairman of the Public Service Commission. He was Joint
Secretary of the Senegal-Gambian Inter-Ministerial Com-
mission in 1961. He became the first Gambian High Commissioner in February 1965.

VAN DER PLAS, CHARLES OLKE. Dutch administrator,
United Nations official, and creator and head of the Gambian Department of Community Development. He first
came to the Gambia in 1954 to make a survey of Gambian

economic and political problems for the United Nations.
He returned to the Gambia in 1963 and convinced the
government to establish the Department of Community Development with minimal financing, and he established his
headquarters at Massembi.

VERMUYDEN, JOHN (Colonel). A servant of the Royal Adventurers who in December 1661 left Elephant Island on
an extended exploration of the upper river areas. His
later report claimed that his expedition penetrated further
into the interior than had Jobson. He claimed to have
passed Jobson's Tenda, the confluence of the Neriko
River, and to have reached beyond the Niololokoba River
before being halted in April 1662 by rapids. Vermuyden
reported that at this point he had discovered a great
amount of gold. He told Prince Rupert of this discovery
and explained that he did not bring out great quantities
for fear of his companions. In 1725, Captain Stibbs re-
traced Vermuyden's journey without discovering the
slightest indication of the fabled gold deposits.

-W-

WALL, JOSEPH (Captain). An Irishman who had served in
the Royal Marines and in the East India Company forces
before joining O'Hara's Corps in the Senegambia in 1773.
After O'Hara's departure in late 1775, Wall served briefly
as Governor of the Senegambia until displaced by Matthias
MacNamara. He was then posted to James Island as
Lieutenant-Governor of the Gambia where his independent
actions and harsh rule caused difficulty with the garrison.
He was ordered imprisoned by MacNamara and spent ten
months in confinement in James Fort before being brought
to trial. In a celebrated case in 1777, Governor MacNamara's allegations against Wall were dismissed and subsequently Wall won two civil cases against the Governor and
the Council of Trade dismissed MacNamara. Wall returned
to the Senegambia and later, while Governor at Goree,
had three soldiers flogged to death. He fled to Europe,
and 20 years later was captured, tried for murder, and
executed.

WALLIKUNDA RICE SCHEME. An attempt on the part of the
Colonial Development Corporation to utilize modern technology

to develop 3400 acres and grow irrigated rice profitably.
In the early 1950s, the corporation sent over 60 construction workers complete with drag lines and bulldozers to
construct irrigation channels, sluices, and a pumping station at Wallikunda. Only 200 acres were ever planted and
the yield was very low, no more than by using the traditional methods. The corporation abandoned the scheme in
1954 except for a small portion of the land which was retained as an experimental station. This ill-conceived venture was even more expensive than the Yundum egg fiasco
and cost the corporation ₤1,115,000.

WESLEYAN MISSION. Its activities in the Gambia date from
February 1821, when John Morgan and his wife arrived
from England. The first attempt at establishing a station
at Mandinari in Kombo was a failure, but the work of an
expanded staff in Bathurst was a success. A mission
house and school were started in 1825, and in 1834, the
present Wesleyan Church was built for the 250-member
congregation. In 1838, the Wesleyans took over 600
acres of land on MacCarthy Island and began a model farm
and agricultural school there. In the early 19th century,
the Wesleyans were particularly effective working with
Liberated Africans. Much of the responsibility for education in the Colony and Protectorate in the early 20th century was assumed by the Wesleyans. In addition to primary schools in Bathurst, they operated a Girls High
School and a Boys High School, and were involved after
1947 in helping to operate the Bathurst School of Science.
In the late 1950s, the two Methodist High Schools were
joined to form the present Bathurst High School.

WEST AFRICAN FIELD FORCE. In 1958 Governor Wyn Harris and his advisors seeking to economize phased out "A"
company of the Sierra Leone Battalion. In March the government created the West African Field Force using the
officers and men from the old company. The Field Force
became a part of the regular police in the Gambia, comprising in the 1960's approximately 140 men or roughly
one-quarter of the entire police force. Men of the Field
Force still continued to be quartered in their old barracks
at Fajara. The force was used primarily for ceremonial
functions and as shock troops to provide for the security
of the capital.

WEST INDIES COMPANY (Dutch). Created by the States
General in 1617 and organized according to Chambers
reflecting the ambitions of the great maritime cities of
Holland. In 1621, the company obtained the Island of
Goree for its base of operations to challenge French
supremacy in Senegambian trade. The company almost
annually sent small ships from Goree to trade along the
Gambia River, but the profit for such ventures was quite
low. In the 1650s, the company at first cooperated with
the Duke of Courland in his Gambia trading venture, but
by 1660 they had seized St. Andrew's Island from him.
Although the island was given back to the Duke's representatives, it was obvious that the Dutch intended to have
it as a base for their Gambian operations. They were
forestalled in this by the actions of Captain Robert Holmes
of the English Royal Adventurers, whose forces took the
island in March 1661 and renamed it James Island. Holmes,
in charge of another expedition, captured Goree from the
Dutch in early 1664, but this station was lost later in the
year when the Dutch Admiral de Ruyter in command of 13
ships arrived in West Africa. De Ruyter, however, by-
passed the English possessions in the Gambia. The Dutch
company thereafter enjoyed a decade of relative supremacy
in the Senegal region. However, the onset of the French
Wars in Europe ended the Dutch interlude in Senegambia.
In 1677, the French Admiral d'Entrées captured Goree and
then drove the Dutch from all their coastal factories. After this, the Dutch company never attempted to challenge
France or Britain in the Senegambia.

WEST INDIES COMPANY (French). A short-lived company
created in 1664 by the all-powerful Minister Colbert. In
a grandiose gesture, he gave the company monopolistic
rights along the shores of the Atlantic Ocean from Canada
to the Cape of Good Hope. His scheme for wresting trade
from the enemies of France by means of this company collapsed in 1672. Trading rights in West Africa were then
assigned to the Senegal Company.

WINDLEY, SIR EDWARD. Governor of the Gambia from 1957
to 1962. He was responsible for introducing the new
Constitution which provided for a greatly expanded House
of Assembly and allowed the elective principle to be applied to the Protectorate in 1960. He made the decision
to appoint Gambians to ministerial positions in the govern-

ment based upon the results of the election, and in 1961
appointed P. S. N'Jie, leader of the United Party, as
Chief Minister.

WOLOF.   One of the most important people of the Senegambia.
They comprise a population in Senegal estimated to be
over three quarters of a million persons with heaviest
concentrations in Walo, Cayor, Jolof, and parts of Baol,
Sine, and Saloum.   In the Gambia, there are approximately 40,000 found mainly in upper and lower Saloum districts
and in the northern sections of Niani, Sami, Niumi, Jokadu,
and also restricted areas of upper Baddibu.   Banjul (Bathurst) is also predominantly a Wolof town, but these have
a different origin than those of the Protectorate since
their ancestors came from the area of Dakar immediately
after the founding of Bathurst.

The Wolof language has been classified by Joseph H.
Greenberg as a part of the northern sub-group of the
Niger-Kordofanian family of languages, and is a commercial language spoken beyond the boundaries of the Senegambia.

Wolof social organization is extremely complex, based
upon a tripartite division of the society into the freeborn,
low-caste persons, and slaves.   Although many modern-
day Wolof are involved in trading and a variety of tasks
associated with modern urban life, most Wolof are agricul-
turalists and live in villages.   The land is divided into
small plots assigned to individuals who practice subsis-
tance agriculture.   Their major cash crop in both Senegal
and the Gambia is groundnuts (peanuts).

Historically, the Wolof states of the Senegambia were
Jolof, Walo, Baol, and Cayor whose rulers (burba, temy,
or damel) controlled their people through a complex bureaucracy combined with armed force.   Those kingdoms
played an important role in temporarily checking the
southward and eastward advance of the French in the
two decades after 1855, but were among the first territories incorporated into the French empire during the
"scramble."   The Wolof in the area of the Gambia Protectorate had not established strong central polities before
the Soninke-Marabout Wars and were politically dependent
upon Mandingo or Serer overlords.

WRIGHT, SIR ANDREW B.   Governor of the Gambia from 1947
to 1949.   Although he was not involved in the planning,

the Colonial Development Corporation made and imple-
mented its decision to invest in the disastrous Yundum
egg scheme and the marginal experimental rice farm at
Wallikunda during his tenure of office. He also had to
frame his budgets with the knowledge that much of the
financing for continued improvements in the economic and
social sphere envisioned by the British government in the
period immediately after World War II would not be forthcoming.

WULI. Located in the extreme upper river area, in the 19th
century it was one of the five north-bank kingdoms controlled by the Mandingo. Founded in the 14th century by
migrants from the Mali Empire, it had become independent
by the time Portuguese traders arrived in the mid-15th
century. Soninke traders travelling between the Gambia,
Senegal, and the Niger River region made Wuli a major
trading area during the long period of the Atlantic slave
trade.
   Throughout the Soninke-Marabout Wars, the rulers of
Wuli maintained a loose client relationship with Bakari
Sardu, the ruler of Bondu, who used the territory as a
corridor and staging ground for his raids into the Gambia.
Despite a number of attempts, Musa Molloh of Fuladu was
never able to add Wuli to his extensive kingdom. The
rulers of Wuli cooperated fully with the various Boundary
Commissions in the 1890s, and Yarbutenda, one of its river
towns, became the terminal point for swinging the arcs
defining the eastern boundary of the Gambia.
   Most of the kingdom was incorporated into the Gambia
by the British although the northern portion became a
part of Senegal. The international frontier dividing the
kingdom and the construction of the railway in Senegal
ruined Wuli's economic position and most of the poor,
sparsely populated area became a District in the 20th-
century reorganization of the Protectorate.

WYN HARRIS, SIR PERCY. Governor of the Gambia from
1949 to 1957. He supervised the minor extensions of political responsibility to allow Colony Gambians a larger
voice in central government decisions. His period in office coincided with growing African nationalist sentiment
in West Africa, and three political parties--the Muslim
Congress, the Democratic Party, and the United Party--
were formed in the Gambia to contest the elections for

the Legislative Council in 1951 and 1954. His disagreements with P. J. N'Jie in 1955 resulted in the leader of
the United Party refusing to serve any further in the
liberalized government of the Colony area. Wyn Harris
launched a modest program for the improvement of Protectorate agriculture. He was particularly interested in
convincing Gambian farmers to increase rice production.
Eventually the agricultural measures he favored helped
to rid the Gambia of its "hungry season."

-Y-

YAMYAMAKUNDA. The site of one of the major Royal African Company factories along the Gambia River. It was
located on the south bank approximately two miles north-
east of the present village of Sankulekunda. The earlier
factory was completely rebuilt by Francis Moore in the
1730s when he was a factor there.

YARBUTENDA. A town in the upper river district of Kantora. According to the Anglo-French Convention of 1889,
Yarbutenda was to be the key to defining the eastern
boundary of the Gambia. The boundary was to be a
radius of ten kilometers drawn with its center at Yarbutenda. The survey commission of 1891 discovered that
the maps of the Gambia were incorrect since there were
two sites which could be considered the town mentioned
in the Convention. Despite further agreements between
the French and British in 1898 and 1901, the eastern
boundary was never satisfactorily determined on the ground.

YUNDUM. A small town in Kombo which during the Soninke-
Marabout Wars was allied with the British. Because of
this and because the chiefs of the town were Soninke, it
was an objective for Fodi Kabba, Fodi Silla, and their
followers. In the late 1940s, it was the site of the disastrous egg scheme sponsored by the British Colonial
Development Corporation. Some of the scheme's abandoned concrete buildings have been incorporated into the
plant of the Gambia Teachers Training College. During
World War II, the allies situated an airfield at Yundum,
and this has since become Gambia's international airport.

YUNDUM COLLEGE. Prior to 1949, all Gambian teachers

received their training either in Sierra Leone or the Gold
Coast. In that year a training center was opened at
Georgetown which offered a one-year course. Most of
the buildings of the defunct egg scheme were acquired
from the Colonial Development Corporation and the Teachers Training College was moved to Yundum in 1952. In
the following year, the course was opened to women, and
in 1954, the program was lengthened to two years. Beginning in 1955, major improvements were made in the
plant and the administration of the college was separated
from the Board of Education and placed under a Board of
Governors.

YUNDUM EGG SCHEME. A plan put into effect by the
Colonial Development Corporation in the Fall of 1948 de-
signed to make the Gambia a major exporter of eggs and
dressed chickens. An initial appropriation of £500,000
was made, and an American poultry expert, Millard Phillips, was appointed field director. The plan was to clear
the bush and timber and sell the wood, and plant the prepared land in grain so that no feed need be imported for
the birds. Permanent poultry houses were built to accommodate enough chickens to provide at maximum production
20 million eggs and one million pounds of poultry per year.
The project was plagued from the start by over optimistic
estimates of the officials of the corporation and the field
staff who ignored the advice of Governor Wright and his
staff. Timber from the cleared site was not of export
quality, and the corporation had difficulty even selling it
for firewood. By October 1950, crop reports showed an
average grain yield of only 207 pounds per acre as compared with estimates of 900 pounds per acre. The poultry, expensive Rhode Island Reds, proved highly sus-
ceptible to fowl pest and died by the thousands. By the
time the Board of Directors of the Corporation agreed in
February 1951 to close the project, it had cost in direct
appropriations £910,000.

BIBLIOGRAPHY

Although there is a considerable body of literature related to the Gambia, the bulk of this material exists as specialized government reports or traveller's accounts. There have been only a few authors who focused upon the Gambia during the explosive period of research and writing on African territories following World War II. Thus, this crucial epoch of political and social ferment has been neglected, and persons concerned with the Gambia are forced to turn to a very fragmented list of books and articles in order to gain some insight into the modern period. To assist the reader in determining the most relevant works, the following bibliography has been selectively annotated. Note that under some "ARTICLES" and "(Government Papers)" sections, in the absence of many author entries, arrangement is chronological.

In order to facilitate the task of finding material on specific subjects, the works have been classified according to the following scheme:

GENERAL
  Exploration/Travel
    Books
      15th-16th Centuries
      17th Century
      18th Century
      19th Century
      20th Century
    Articles
  Guides
    Pamphlets
    Articles

CULTURAL
  Literature
  Linguistic
  Press

ECONOMIC
  Agriculture
    Books
    Gambia Gov. Reports
    G.B. Colonial Off. Rpts.

  Development
    Gambia Gov. Reports
    G.B. Papers
    Articles
  Finance
    Gambia Gov. Reports
    Misc. Reports
  Labor
    Gambia Gov. Reports
    Articles
  Transport
    Gambia Gov. Reports

HISTORICAL
  15th-19th Centuries
    Books
    G.B. Colonial Off. Papers
  20th Century
    Books
    Articles

POLITICAL
  Constitution

Gambia Gov. Papers
G.B. Papers
Articles
Government
Books
Gambia Gov. Papers
Articles
Gambia Gov. Ordinances
Law
Political Parties
Foreign Affairs
G.B. Papers
Articles

SCIENTIFIC
Geography

Books
Articles
Geology
Medicine
Natural Science

SOCIAL
Anthropology/Archaeology
Books
Articles
Demography
Gambia Gov. Reports
Education
Gambia Gov. Reports
Religion
Sociology

GENERAL: EXPLORATION AND TRAVEL

BOOKS

15th and 16th Centuries

Asseline, David. Les Antiquités et chroniques de la ville de Dieppe,
2 vols. (Dieppe: 1874).

Hakluyt, Richard. Principal Navigations of the English Nation,
5 vols. (London: 1927). See particularly Vol. IV, pp. 285 &
Vol. V, pp. 44-52.

Hakluyt Society. The Voyages of Cadamosto and other Documents on
Western Africa in the Second Half of the 15th Century (London:
1937). Cadamosto, the discoverer of the Gambia River for Prince
Henry, in the journals of his two voyages of the mid-15th century
gives the first reliable European account of the river and its inhabitants.

Monod, Theodore, ed. Description de la Côte Occidentale d'Afrique
par Valentin Fernandes (1506-1510) (Paris: 1938), pp. 25-27.
One of the earliest European accounts of the tribal dispositions
near the coastline of Senegambia.

17th Century

Barbot, Jean. Description of the Coasts of North and South Guinea
(London: 1732). The first edition of this work was prepared some
time in the 1680s. See particularly p. 70 ff.

Cultru, Prosper. Premier Voyage de Sieur de la Courbe (Paris: 1918).

Jobson, Richard. The Golden Trade (London: 1932). Jobson was sent out as supercargo on a trading expedition by the Royal Adventurers of England in 1620 to relieve a previous expedition and to carry on trade with the natives on the river. He and others proceeded upriver as far as Barrakunda Falls. Although their trading exports did not result in a profit for the company, Jobson's notes and comments form a classic of African travel.

Le Maire, M. Voyage to the Canaries, Cape Verd and the Coast of Africa under the Command of M. Dancourt, 1682 (Edinburgh: 1887). See particularly pp. 35-60. An excellent description is given of the remains of the Portuguese influence in the river on p. 47. The first publication of this work was in Paris in 1695.

Perrot, Nicolas. L'Afrique de Marmol--de la traduction de Nicolas Perrot, 3 vols. (Paris: 1667). See Vol. III, pp. 70-90.

Rochefort, Jannequin de. Voyage de Libye au Royaume Genega (Paris: 1643).

Stibbs, Capt. B. Journal of a Voyage up the Gambia (London: 1732). Stibbs was the sub-commander of James Island who undertook an exploratory voyage to the upper Gambia in 1724. This Journal relates his experiences and observations. His reports of native stories of vast riches in the further interior helped to create the myth of the secret gold mines that motivated many 18th-century traders. The Journal is also reproduced in Francis Moore's Travels.

Thevenot, Melchisedech. Memoires du voyage aux Indes Orientales du Général Beaulieu (Paris: 1672). Contains a description of the first attempt by the French to settle a colony and build a fort on the Gambia River in 1612.

Warburton, Eliot. Memoirs of Prince Rupert and the Cavaliers, 3 vols. (London: 1849). Vol. 3 is the most pertinent for the Gambia since it contains the record of Prince Rupert's activities on the Gambia River directed against the Commonwealth including the sacking of Bintang. Rupert also reported tales of a mountain of pure gold located somewhere in the upper river area.

18th Century

Adanson, M. A Voyage to Senegal, the Isle of Goree and the River Gambia (London: 1759). Observations made by a French naturalist who visited the Senegambia in 1749. See particularly pp. 156-172 for description of coastal tribes.

Astley, Thomas. A New General Collection of Voyages and Travels, 4 vols. (London: 1745). Vols. 1 and 2 contain many of the older travel accounts--Cadamosto, Barbot, de Rochefort, Le Maire, and others. As such, because the originals are hard to obtain, it is one of the most valuable composite works dealing with West Africa.

Blagdon, Francis. Modern Discoveries (London: 1802). Vols. 3 and 4 contain S. M. X. Golbery, "Fragments d'un voyage en Afrique (1785-1787)." The most important section of Blagdon's work is the translation of Golbery's observations made between the years 1785-87. Golbery served the French in the Senegambia for a number of years, and his work is particularly useful for details of French trading ventures there.

Churchill, John. A Collection of Voyages (London: 1744). Contains older accounts such as Courbe and Barbot.

Golbery, Silvanius Meinrad Xavier. Fragments d'un voyage en Afrique (1785-1787), 2 vols. (Paris: 1802).

Labat, Jean Baptiste. Nouvelle relation de l'Afrique Occidentale, 5 vols. (Paris: 1728). Particularly Vol. 1, pp. 304-307; Vol. 4, pp. 256-264, 367-380; Vol. 5, pp. 2-22, 307-324. This is an account of the travels and policies of Andre Brue who was sent out in 1697 to Goree to be Director General of the French Senegal Company. See particularly Vol. 1, pp. 304-307 and Vol. 5, pp. 2-22 and 307-324 for tribal alignments and customs in the Gambia.

Moore, Francis. Travels in the Inland Part of Africa (London: 1738). Moore was a scholarly young man sent by the Royal African Company to be a "writer" at James Island in 1730. He survived four years and left behind a monumental work of observation concerning peoples, customs, trade, insects, and animals which also contains very lucid insights into social and political organizations. This work read in conjunction with Jobson also shows how much had changed in the Gambia in the course of a century. Also appended to Moore's notes is Stibbs, Journal of an earlier exploratory voyage.

Park, Mungo. Travels in the Interior Districts of Africa (London: 1899). The Travels are concerned with the Gambia only to the extent that Park used the Gambia as his point of departure and he did describe the people of the Gambia very vividly. He left Pisania (Karantaba) in December 1795 after a six-month stay at the home of Dr. Laidley. His observations of local customs and color are matched only by Francis Moore's writings.

Smith, William. A New Voyage to Guinea (London: 1744). See p. 32 ff. for a description of Smith's visit to the Gambia in 1726-27.

Walckenaer, Charles Athanase. Collections des relations de voyages
    par mer et par terre en différentes parties de l'Afrique, 2 vols.
    (Paris: 1842).

19th Century

Alexander, James E. Narrative of a Voyage of Observation Among
    the Colonies of West Africa, 2 vols. (London: 1853). A good
    account of Bathurst and prospects of tapping interior trade from
    there is given in Vol. 1, pp. 70-72.

Biller, Sarah. Memoir of Hannah Kilham (London: 1837). Mrs.
    Kilham, a member of the Society of Friends, was one of the
    earliest missionaries to the Gambia. She began studying Wolof
    and preparing school books before going to the Gambia in 1823.

Bowdich, T. E. Excursions in Maderia and Porto Santa, to which
    is added ... "A description of the English Settlements on the
    River Gambia" by Mrs. Bowdich, (London: 1825). Mrs. Bow-
    dich's account of the Gambia begins on p. 204.

[Burton, Richard F.] "An F.R.G.S." Wanderings in West Africa,
    2 vols. (London: 1863). The famous explorer and Islamic
    scholar spent a few days in the vicinity of Bathurst and left a
    rather negative traveller's version of the worthlessness of the
    Gambia.

Ellis, A. B. The Land of Fetish (London: 1883). A very super-
    ficial account by an officer who was stationed in the Gambia for
    a brief time. For his impressions of the Gambia see pp. 1-34.

Gaunt, Mary. Alone in West Africa (London: 1912). Chapter 2
    contains her impressions of the Gambia.

Gray, Major William. Travels in Western Africa in the Years 1819-
    1821 from the River Gambia, thru Woolli, Bondoo, Galam, Kassan,
    Kaarta and Foolidoo to the River Niger (London: 1825). See
    particularly p. 46 ff. and pp. 192-194.

Hewitt, J. F. Napier. European Settlements on the West Coast of
    Africa (London: 1862). Hewitt was a more than usually pre-
    judiced observer of the British administration of the Gambia.
    Provides a counterbalance to the more favorable reports by
    other 19th-century travellers.

Huntley, Sir Henry. Seven Years' Service on the Slave Coast of
    Western Africa, 2 vols. (London: 1850). Huntley was the third
    Lieutenant-Governor of the Gambia, assuming his post in 1840.
    Considering the important administrative problems of the Gambia
    at that time, this work is remarkably noninformative. Primarily
    useful as a traveller's account.

Mitchinson, A. W. The Expiring Continent, A Narrative of Travel in the Senegambia, etc. (London: 1881). A travel book.

Mollien, G. Travels in the Interior of Africa to the Sources of the Senegal and Gambia in the Year 1818, ed. T. E. Bowdich, (London: 1820). The work deals primarily with Mollien's explorations and is of slight value for the Gambia except in the reports of the customs of people of the same tribe as those who lived in the Gambia Valley.

Morgan, John. Reminiscences of the Founding of a Christian Mission on the Gambia (London: 1864). Contains some brief glimpses into the life and customs of the Wolof and Mandingo people.

Park, Mungo. Journal of a Mission to the Interior of Africa in the Year 1805 (London: 1815). On his ill-fated second journey in 1805, Park also left from Pisania, and it was to this place that his interpreter, Issaco, brought the Journal. The Journal, although a necessary supplement to the earlier Travels, has even less to say about the Gambia.

Poole, T. E. Life, Scenery & Customs in Sierra Leone and the Gambia, 2 vols. (London: 1850). Poole was Colonial and Garrison Chaplain of Sierra Leone from 1845-50. His impressions of the Gambia are in Vol. 2, pp. 70-85; 138-140, and 205 ff.

Rançon, A. Dans la Haute-Gambie. Voyage d'exploration scientifique, 1891-1892 (Paris: 1894). Valuable only as a corollary account of areas adjacent to the Gambia.

Reade, W. Winwood. Savage Africa (London: 1864). A naive and superficial account of the Senegambia is in Chapters 30-33.

Whitford, John. Trading Life in Western and Central Africa (London: 1877). See pp. 18-22 for the Gambia.

Wilson, J. L. Western Africa, Its History Conditions and Prospects (London: 1856).

Wood, J. Dobson. To West Africa and Back (London: 1894). A general travel account of a trip to Gambia and the Canary Islands.

20th Century

Crowder, Michael. Pagans and Politicians (London: 1959). The book was a result of a journey made by the author immediately after his university training--not a typical European voyage, but one on the cheap. Crowder met the people on their own level. Pp. 25-43 represents his impression of the Gambia.

Gamble, David. A General Bibliography of the Gambia. Boston:
G. K. Hall & Co., 1979. The most complete bibliography available of works of all types related to the Senegambia region. Up
to date as of 1972.

Gunther, John. Inside Africa (New York: 1955). Little inside
information is to be found on pp. 742-745.

Hardinge, R. Gambia and Beyond (London: 1934). A brief superficial travel account.

Hempstone, Smith. Africa, Angry Young Giant (New York: 1961).
Pp. 359-392 deals with the Gambia. Hempstone is not just a
casual traveller, and in one brief chapter he shows considerable
insight into the society and modern problems of the Gambia.

Rice, Berkeley. Enter Gambia, The Birth of an Improbable Nation
(Boston: 1967). Rice's improbable book, despite its lack of or-
ganization, is quite valuable in recording his impressions of the
Gambian scene during the period immediately after independence.

Willis, Colin. White Traveller in Black Africa (London: 1951). The
author is a most intelligent, journalistic observer of the African
scene. Chapter 10 concerns the Gambia.

ARTICLES

Hadson, H. "Golden Gambia," Travel, Jan. 1957, pp. 52-54.

MacColl, R. "Gambia, The Colony Nobody Knows," Atlantic, May
1962, pp. 108-112.

Phillips, R. H. "Up River through the Gambia," Crown Colonist,
1933, pp. 249-50.

Porter, Sibyl. "Gambia Journey," West African Review, April 1952,
pp. 330-32. Story of a ten-day trek through the Gambia Protectorate.

Rice, B. "Enter Gambia, Laughing," Harpers, Oct. 1966, pp. 74-78.

Van der Plas, C. O. "Discovering the Gambia," United Nations
Review, Dec. 1958, pp. 15-19.

GENERAL: GUIDES

PAMPHLETS

<u>The Gambia</u> (London, 1967).

<u>The Gambia ... in Brief</u> (Portsmouth, 1967).   Both of these were
   issued by the Gambian Government as aids for tourists.

ARTICLES

Gailey, Harry A. "African Archives--Gambia," <u>Africana Newsletter</u>,
   Vol. I, no. 3, 1963.

_____. "Bibliographic Essays--The Gambia," <u>Africana Newsletter</u>,
   Vol. II, no. 1, 1964.

CULTURAL: LITERATURE

There have been few literary works whose locale was the Gambia,
and the two most successful authors born in the territory have
chosen to write in generalized African terms. The action in William
Conton's <u>The African</u> takes place in an area obviously not the Gambia. Lenrie Peters, one of the finest modern poets, addresses his
audience in more universal terms. The only novels which refer
specifically to the Gambia are: John Bingley, <u>Mr. Khoury</u> (London:
1952) and Margery Lawrence, <u>The Gilded Jar</u> (London: 1948).

CULTURAL: LINGUISTICS

Faye, J. C., and M. A. Sillah. <u>The Orthography of Gambian
   Languages--Wolof and Mandinka</u> (Bathurst: 1956).

Gamble, D. P. <u>Mandinka Reading Book</u> (Bathurst: 1956).

_____. <u>Notes on Mandinka</u> (Bathurst: 1949).

Hopkinson, Emilius. <u>Mandingo Vocabulary</u> (1911, with addenda
   1924).

MacBrian, the Rev. R. M. <u>A Grammar of the Mandingo Language
   with Vocabularies</u> (London: 1937).

Nunn, G. N. N. A Short Phrase Book and Classified Vocabulary
    from English into Mandinka (Bathurst: 1934).

O'Halloran, G., and F. Sidible. Mandinka Talibe la Kitabo (Bat-
    hurst: 1948).

Rowlands, E. C. A Grammar of Gambian Mandinka (London: 1959).

CULTURAL: PRESS

Gambia Echo, weekly.

Gambia News Bulletin, published three times a week by the Gambia
    Government Information Service.

Kibaro. Issued monthly in late 1940s by the Senior Commissioner,
    Marina, Bathurst. Written in Mandinka language in Roman script.

The Nation, monthly.

News Gambia, weekly.

ECONOMIC: AGRICULTURE

BOOKS

Dawe, M. T. Report on the Agricultural Conditions and Needs of
    the Gambia (Bathurst: 1921).

Dudgeon, G. G. The Agricultural and Forest Products of British
    West Africa (London: 1911). For the Gambia see pp. 1-14.

Moloney, A. Sketch of the Forestry of West Africa (London: 1887).

GAMBIA GOVERNMENT REPORTS

Brooks, A. J. "The Cultivation of Groundnuts," Department of
    Agriculture Bulletin #3 (1929).

Palmer, J. H. "Notes on Strange Farmers," Sessional Paper #15
    (1946).

Pirie, J. "Vegetable Cultivation. Hints to Protectorate Farmers," Department of Agriculture Bulletin #3 (1929).

Rodden, G. M. "A Report of Rice Cultivation in the Gambia," Sessional Paper #2 (1943).

Roe, C. J. "Report on Swamp Reclamation and the Improvements of Existing Rice Lands by Drainage, Irrigation, etc., in the Gambia," Sessional Paper #1 (1943).

Rosevear, D. R. "Report on the Forest Conditions of the Gambia" (1936).

Van der Plas, C. O. "Report of a Survey of Rice Areas in the Central Division of the Gambia Protectorate" (August 1955).

_____. "A Summary of the Conclusions and Recommendations of the Conference on Cooperative Societies held at University College, Ibadan, 13-17 December 1954" (1955).

Agriculture Department Report. Annual, from 1924.

Forestry Department Annual Report. From 1950. Issued as Sessional Papers of the Legislative Council.

Gambia Oilseeds Marketing Board. Annual Report. From 1949-50.

Gambian Rice Farm. Annual Report.

GREAT BRITAIN, COLONIAL OFFICE REPORTS

Haswell, M. R. Economics of Agriculture in a Savannah Village, 1953.

_____. The Changing Pattern of Economic Activity in a Gambian Village, 1963.

ECONOMIC: DEVELOPMENT

GAMBIA GOVERNMENT REPORTS

Blackburne, K. W., et al. "Development and Welfare in the Gambia" (1943).

"Report of a Committee Appointed to Consider Remedial Measures

to be Adopted to Deal with Over-crowding in Bathurst"
(1946).

"Correspondence with the Secretary of State for the Colonies on
the Replanning of Bathurst and the Development of Kombo,"
Sessional Paper #1 (1944).

"Secretary of State's Reply to the Second Application for Assistance
under C. D. W. Act for Bathurst/Kombo," Sessional Paper #12
(1945).

"Exploration for Petroleum Deposits in Gambia," Sessional Paper #6
(1959).

"Gambian Government, Development Plan, 1964-67," Sessional Paper
#10 (1964).

"Revision of the Development Programme 1964-67," Sessional Paper
#1 (1966).

"Gambia Government, 1967-68 to 1970-71," Sessional Paper #4 (1967).

GREAT BRITAIN, PAPERS BY COMMAND

"Statement of Policy on Colonial Development and Welfare," Cmd.
6175 (Feb. 1940).

"Report on the Gambian Egg Scheme," Cmd. 8560.

ARTICLES

Crowder, M. "'Chicken Coop' College--Aftermath of the Gambia Egg
Farm," West African Review, 1956.

Ivor, Thomas. "Lessons of Gambia Poultry Farm," New Commonwealth, August 1951, pp. 88-89.

Momoh, Eddie. "The Gambia: Struggle for Recovery," West
Africa, 9 January 1984, pp. 60-61.

_____. "Gambia Budget: Sisay's Medicine," West Africa, 25
July 1983, pp. 1704-1705.

"Rehousing and Townplanning in the Gambia," West African Review,
Oct. 1946, pp. 1123-24.

"Bathurst Drainage and Reclamation Work," New Commonwealth,
1947, pp. 605-606.

"Gambia Chicken Farm," West African Review, Dec. 1948, p. 1423.

"Gambia's Georgia Man--M. J. Phillips," CDC., West Africa, 3 June 1950, p. 485.

"CDC Statement on the Gambian Egg Scheme," West Africa, 21 April 1951, p. 357.

"Lord Trefgarne on the Gambia Poultry Scheme," West Africa, 21 April 1951, p. 351.

ECONOMIC: FINANCE

GAMBIA GOVERNMENT REPORTS

"Report of Commission to Investigate and Report on the Financial Position of the Colony" (1953).

"Statement of Government Policy Regarding Groundnut Prices and the Use of a Stabilization Fund and Kindred Matters, 1955" (1955).

"The Financial Position--Exchange of Despatches Between the Government and Secretary of State for the Colonies," Sessional Paper #11 (1960).

Loynes, J. B. "Report on the Problem of the Future Currencies of Sierra Leone and the Gambia," Sessional Paper #12 (1961).

"Account General, Financial Report with Appendices, 1964," Sessional Paper #9 (1966).

"Address of the Governor-General at the Budget Session of the House of Representatives, 22 June 1967," Sessional Paper #5 (1967).

"British Financial Aid to the Gambia, 1967/68 to 1970/71," Sessional Paper #7 (1967).

MISCELLANEOUS REPORTS

Great Britain, Cmd. 1600. "Report of a Committee on Trade and Taxation for British West Africa" (1922).

International Labour Organisation. "Expanded Programme of

Technical Assistance-Report to Government of the Gambia on Cooperative Banking" (1964).

_____. "Expanded Programme of Technical Assistance-Second Report to Government of the Gambia on Cooperative Banking" (1965).

United States. Bureau of Foreign Commerce. "Import Tariff System of Gambia" World Trade Information Service Operation Report (61-33), (April 1961).

ECONOMIC: LABOR

GAMBIA GOVERNMENT REPORTS

"Commission to Investigate the Basic Terms and Conditions of Daily rated Labour," Sessional Paper #2 (1959).

ARTICLES

Gailey, Harry A. "Fixing the Rate for Gambia Jobs," West Africa, Feb. 11, 1961, p. 151.

_____. "Portrait, Gambia's Labour Leader," West Africa, May 17, 1961, p. 569.

_____. "Jallow's Progress," Portrait, West Africa, May 2, 1964, p. 481.

"New Act on Wages in Gambia," International Labour Review, Oct. 1966, p. 416.

ECONOMIC: TRANSPORT

GAMBIA GOVERNMENT REPORTS

"Report of a Committee Appointed to Enquire into the Conduct and Management of the River Steamer Service," Sessional Paper #11 (1944).

"Report of the Committee Appointed to Consider Remedial Measures

to be Adopted to Deal with Overcrowding in Bathurst," Sessional
Paper #18 (1946).

HISTORICAL: 15TH-19TH CENTURIES

BOOKS

Archer, F. Bisset.   The Gambia Colony and Protectorate (London:
    1906).   The author was a former civil servant in the Gambia and
    the book's strengths and weaknesses reflect his primary vocation.
    It is a mine of factual information concerning British activities in
    the Gambia in the 19th century.

Blake, J. W.   European Beginnings in West Africa (London: 1937).
    This work, in combination with those of Davies and Martin,
    serves as an excellent introduction to the early history of
    Europeans in western Africa.

Cultru, Prosper.   Histoire du Sénégal (Paris: 1910).   An older
    work that still remains in many ways the best history of Senegal.

Curtin, Philip D.   Economic Change in Pre Colonial Africa: Sene-
    gambia in the Era of the Slave Trade, 2 vol., Madison: Univer-
    sity of Wisconsin Press, 1975.

Davies, K. G.   The Royal African Company (London: 1957).   The
    Royal African Company played the most important role in the
    British trading spheres in West Africa for almost a century.
    Davies' work is invaluable in evaluating the nature and scope
    of British activities.   The Senegambia was considered a minor
    arena for their trading operations.   Most of the book is devoted
    to the more economically viable areas.   Nevertheless, anyone
    dealing with the Senegambia must consult at least the pertinent
    sections of this book.

Deschamps, Hubert.   Le Sénégal et la Gambie (Paris: 1964).

Diederich, Heinrich.   Herzog Jakobs von Kurland Kolonien an der
    Westkuste von Afrika (Miltau: 1890).   This book is still useful
    for a background to the Courlander experiment, although it has
    largely been supplanted by Mattiesen.

Eckert, Walter.   Kurland unter dem Einfluss des Merkantilismus,
    1551-1682 (Riga: 1927).   Contains an excellent if somewhat
    dated account of the Courlander's colonizing efforts in the 17th
    century.

Fitzgerald, H. E. The Gambia and Its Proposed Cession to France
(London: 1875). A brief panegyric on the question of exchanging the Gambia.

Gray, Sir John M. A History of the Gambia (Cambridge: 1940;
reprinted London: 1966). Gray was a former Justice in the
Gambian Supreme Court and, as his later works on East Africa
attest, an accomplished scholar. This history is probably the
best single volume work every published on the Gambia. Sir
John utilized archival materials both in England and the Gambia.
The work is particularly useful in detailing the early trade rivalries of the European powers and for the intricate patterns of
African conflicts in the 19th century. It is, however, not an
interpretive work and further, it is not concerned with the 20th
century developments in the Senegambia.

Hamlyn, W. T. A Short History of the Gambia (Bathurst: 1931).
This is a very short non-detailed secondary school textbook
which was brought up to date through World War II by Hamlyn
with the publication of Stories of the Gambia (Bathurst: 1945).

Klein, Martin. Islam and Imperialism in Senegal (Stanford: 1968).
The sections pp. 63-113 give the best detailed description of
Ma Bâ and the Soninke-Marabout conflict.

Lawrence, A. W. Trade Castles and Forts of West Africa (London:
1963). Contains good descriptions of the building of early European forts in the Senegambia. See particularly pp. 250-261 for
James Fort.

Martin, Evelyne. The British West Africa Settlements 1750-1821
(London: 1927). Martin's work is complementary to that of
Davies. The years involved in this study cover the transition
period from rule by the Royal African Company to the assumption of direct control by the Crown.

Mattiesen, Otto Heinz. Die Kolonial und Uberseepolitik der kur-
landischen Herzöge im 17 und 18 Jahrhundert (Stuttgart: 1940).
This is one of the most difficult works to obtain which treat of
European colonization in the 17th century. It is the finest work
on the subject of Courland's short-lived colonial experiments in
Africa and the West Indies. The long scholarly discussion on
their efforts in the Senegambia is particularly well done.

Palmer, H. R. The Carthaginian Voyage to West Africa (Bathurst:
1931). Palmer was a governor of the Gambia who had served
many years in Nigeria. He was a very good amateur historian
and linguist. The first portion of this book deals with the
probability that Hanno, the Carthaginian sailor, reached the
Senegambia.

Pfeffer, Karl Heinz. Sierra Leone and Gambia (Bonn: 1958).
   This is a short generalized work on the two British African
   territories.

Quinn, Charlotte A. Mandingo Kingdoms of the Senegambia: Tra-
   ditionalism, Islam and European Expansion. Evanston, Ill:
   Northwestern University Press, 1972.

_____. "Mandingo States in Nineteenth Century Gambia" in
   Carleton T. Hodge, ed., Papers on Manding (Bloomington, Ind.:
   1971). This is the best detailed coverage of the organization,
   development and conflict of Gambian Mandingo states during this
   crucial period.

Reeve, Henry F. The Gambia (London: 1912).   Reeve was another
   civil servant in the Gambia.   His book is well written and is not
   only a political history, but contains a description of peoples,
   languages, customs, and the flora and fauna of the area.   Not-
   withstanding the undeveloped state of anthropological knowledge
   at that time, Reeve shows some excellent insights.   Read together
   with Gray's History, it becomes an invaluable secondary work.

Sabatie, A. Le Sénégal, sa conquête et son organisation, 1364-
   1925 (Paris: 1962).   One of the better organized accounts of
   French activity in the Senegambia.   It contains much useful material on all periods of French interest in the Gambia.   It is a
   particularly good presentation of the French point of view in the
   crucial years 1880-1900.

Verdier, A. Exchange de Territoire Coloniale (La Rochelle: 1876).
   A pamphlet opposing the exchange of territory in West Africa
   with Britain.

Young, Frederick, et al. Report of the Council of the Royal Colonial Institute on the Gambia Question (London: 1876).   Issued
   to convince the government that the Gambia was valuable and
   should not be traded.

ARTICLES

Brooks, George. "Peanuts and Colonialism.   Consequences of the
   Commercialization of Peanuts in West Africa, 1830-70," Journal
   of African History, Vol. 16, No. 1, 1975.

Currey, E. Hamilton. "Boat Actions and River Fights--The
   Baddiboo War," United Service Magazine, Vol. 49, 1914, pp.
   124-133.

Gray, John. "Zimmerman's 18th Century Gambia Journey," African
   Affairs, Feb. 1959, pp. 65-74.

Harden, D. B. "The Phoenicians on the West Coast of Africa,"
Antiquity, Sept. 1948, pp. 141-150.

Macklin, B. W. "Queens and Kings of Niumi," Man, May 1935.

Mahoney, Florence K. "African Leadership in Bathurst in the
Nineteenth Century," Tarikh, Vol. 2, No. 2, 1968.

Quinn, Charlotte. "Maba Diakhou Bâ, Scholar-Warrior of the
Senegambia," Tarikh, Vol. 2, No. 3, 1968.

_____. "A Nineteenth Century Fulbe State," Journal of African
History, Vol. 12, No. 3, 1971, pp. 427-440.

Sillah, M. B. "The Demise of Kings," West Africa, 6 June 1983,
pp. 1351-53.

Southorn, Lady Bella. "James Island," West African Review, May
1949, pp. 484-489, pp. 506-507 (photographs).

Southorn, Sir Wilfred Thomas. "Earliest British Settlement in
Africa," Crown Colonist, 1943, pp. 391-392.

Stein, Robert. "Mortality in the eighteenth Century Slave Trade,"
Journal of African History, Vol. 21, No. 1, 1980.

Swindell, Ken. "SeraWoolies, Tillibunkas and Strange Farmers:
The Development of Migrant Groundnut Farming along the Gambia
River, 1848-95," Journal of African History, Vol. 21, No. 1,
1980.

Wood, W. Raymond. "An Archaeological Appraisal of Early European
Settlements in the Senegambia," The Journal of African History,
Vol. 8, No. 1, 1967, pp. 39-64.

GREAT BRITAIN, COLONIAL OFFICE PAPERS

"A Reply of the Merchants of the Gambia to the Despatches of Sir
Arthur Kennedy," West African Pamphlet #1 (1870).

"Correspondence Relating to the Territories on the River Gambia,"
African #348 (1887).

"Correspondence Relating to British and French Jurisdiction,"
African #377 (1890).

"Correspondence Relating to the Gambian Expedition" (1901). The
details of the joint French-English expedition against Fodi Kabba
and Musa Molloh.

HISTORICAL: 20TH CENTURY

BOOKS

Gailey, Harry A. A History of the Gambia (London: 1964). Although the history of the Gambia before 1900 is summarized, the main emphasis of this work is upon 20th-century developments to the eve of independence. It is the only detailed treatment of the Gambia in the 20th century.

Great Britain. Foreign Office. Historical Section. Peace Handbooks (London: 1920). Vol. 15, No. 91 contains a brief survey of the Gambia; Vol. 17, No. 102 reports in a simple fashion concerning the Senegal.

Huxley, Elspeth. Four Guineas (London: 1954). Chapter 1 is devoted to the Gambia. This is certainly one of the lesser works by this very gifted observer of Africa. She stayed only a few days in the Gambia and this combined with her East African background enabled her to draw a large number of wrong conclusions.

Schramm, Joseph. Gambia (Bonn: 1965). This is a very short, simple pamphlet.

Southorn, Lady Bella. The Gambia (London: 1952). A very interesting book written by the wife of a former governor. Lady Southorn's book depends largely upon personal observation and the factual underpinning of Reeve and Gray. It is a combination history and eyewitness account which because of her skill renders the people and customs more alive than any work on the Gambia written in the 20th century.

Welch, Claude. Dream of Unity (Ithaca, N.Y.: 1966). The section pp. 250-292 contains an excellent discussion of the background to an early development of the movement for a united Senegambia.

ARTICLES

Armitage, Capt. C. H. "The Gambia Colony and Protectorate," Journal of the Royal Society of Arts, 22 June 1928, pp. 811-818.

Langley, M. "Gambia: Trading Post to Independent Nation," History Today, June 1965, pp. 420-425.

POLITICAL: CONSTITUTION

GAMBIA GOVERNMENT, SPECIALIZED PUBLICATIONS

Consultative Committee on the Constitution.   "Report.   1953,"
    Gazette, Vol. 70, July 31, 1953.

"An Act to Establish and Make Provisions for the Constitution of
    the Gambia," The Gazette (Supplement), No. 4, Nov. 1969.

"Proposed Constitutional Changes in the Gambia," Sessional Paper
    #27 (1953).

"Constitutional Development in the Gambia," Sessional Paper #4
    (1959).

"Constitutional Development in the Gambia," Sessional Paper #6
    (1961).

GREAT BRITAIN, SPECIALIZED PUBLICATIONS

Central Office of Information.   Constitutional Progress in the
    Gambia, 1955.

Cmnd. 1468.   "Report of Gambian Constitutional Conference" (1961).

Cmnd. 2435.   "The Gambia Independence Conference" (1964).

ARTICLES

Gailey, Harry A.   "What Next in the Gambia," West Africa, Part I,
    22 July 1961, p. 801; Part II, 29 July 1961, p. 861.

"Gambia and Malta," West Africa, 11 Jan. 1958, p. 25.

"Independence Aim," New Commonwealth, Dec. 1960, p. 809.

Land, Harry.   "What Status for Sierra Leone and Gambia," New
    Commonwealth, Sept. 1960, pp. 568-570.

"Universal Suffrage for the Gambia," New Commonwealth, Oct, 1959,
    pp. 683-684.

POLITICAL: GOVERNMENT

BOOKS

Hailey, (Lord).   Native Administration in the British African Territories, 4 vols. (London: 1950).   Vol. III, pp. 329-350 treats
in great detail the instruments of the Gambia government
through 1951.

Hertslet, Sir Edward.   Map of Africa by Treaty (London: 1894).
An invaluable work, particularly for the historian of late 19th-
century Africa.   Hertslet has reproduced the major treaties between the great powers and also those between the European
states and major native rulers.

GAMBIA GOVERNMENT, SPECIALIZED
PUBLICATIONS

"Instructions for the Guidance of Commissioners" (1936).

"Political Memoranda for the Guidance of Commissioners and Other
Government Officers Working in the Protectorate" (1933).

"Some Aspects of Local Government," Foreword by Sir Hilary Blood
(1946).

"Report of the Committee on the Legislative Council Franchise,"
Sessional Paper #2 (1944).

"Report of the Bathurst Temporary Local Authority for the Year
1945," Sessional Paper #9 (1946).

"Report of the Constituency Boundaries Commission," Sessional
Paper #2 (1966).

"Instructions for the Travelling Commissioners of the Gambia,"
West African Pamphlet #125 (1923).

ARTICLES

Crowder, Michael.   "Chiefs in Gambia Politics," West Africa, Part I,
18 Oct. 1958, p. 987; Part II, 25 Oct. 1958, p. 1017.

_____.   "Seyfou Omar M'Baki--Portrait," West Africa, 8 April
1961.

Gailey, Harry A.   "Gambia Chiefs' Question," West Africa, 11 March
    1961, p. 255.

Hughes, Arnold.   "Why the Gambian Coup Failed," West Africa
    pt. 1, 20 Oct. 1981, pp. 2498-2502, pt. 2, 2 Nov. 1981, pp.
    2570-2573.

Nyang, Sulayman.   "The Gambia After the Rebellion," African Re-
    port, Nov.-Dec. 1981.

"Government Confers with Chiefs in the Gambia," New Common-
    wealth, 6 July 1953, pp. 27-29.

"Gambia's Critical Period," West Africa, 16 May 1964, p. 546.

"The Last Governor," Portrait, Sir John Paul, West Africa, 22
    August 1964, p. 939.

"The Gambia's Number Two," Portrait, Sherif Sisay, West Africa,
    31 Oct. 1964, p. 1219.

"New Voice from Africa" (Jawara), West Africa, 13 Feb. 1965, p.
    173.

"The Gambia's High Commissioner" (Louis Valentine), West Africa,
    20 Feb. 1965, p. 197.

"Newest, Smallest: Gambia Gains Independence," Time, 26 Feb.
    1965, p. 32.

"Toward the Gambia Republic," West Africa, 25 Sept., p. 1025 and
    2 Oct. 1965, p. 1110.

"The Republic Rejected," West Africa, 4 Dec. 1965, pp. 1386-1387.

"The Gambian in Government House," Portrait, Farimang Singhateh,
    West Africa, 30 April 1966, p. 477.

"Restabilising the Gambia," West Africa, 10 Aug. 1981, pp. 1805-
    1806.

GAMBIA GOVERNMENT, SELECTED ORDINANCES

#11 (1894) Protectorate Ordinance.
    The Basic government ordinance which established indirect rule
in the Protectorate remained in force subject to changes by Amendment Ordinances until 1913. However, even after being officially
supplanted, this Ordinance remained the key for the future theoretical development of Protectorate Administration.

#7 (1895) Protectorate Yard Tax Ordinance.
First defined a yard as the basic unit of taxation for the Protectorate and established scales of taxation.

#6 (1896) Protectorate Land Ordinance.
The basic ordinance that governed all Protectorate lands, except Public Lands, until 1945. All lands to be held by the native authorities and administered by them for the good of the people of a district.

#4 (1897) Protectorate Land (Amendment) Ordinance.
Vested the administration of Public Lands in the Chiefs and Headmen of the Protectorate.

#7 (1902) Protectorate Ordinance.
Brought Fuladu, previously controlled by Mussa Molloh, under the Protectorate system. Also extended the system to British Kombo. Otherwise the Ordinance was a repeat of #11, 1894.

#11 (1909) Protectorate (Amendment) Ordinance.
The most important amendment to #7, 1902 gave the native tribunals jurisdiction over all natives of West Africa resident in a given district.

#13 (1909) Protectorate (Amendment) Ordinance.
Main amendment concerned the appointment and regulation of badge messengers for the Chiefs.

#30 (1913) Protectorate Ordinance.
Repealed all previous Protectorate Ordinances and consolidated them along with Rules and Regulations made by the Governor in Council, into one all inclusive ordinance.

#10 (1915) Protectorate (Amendment) Ordinance.
Redefined and clarified the executive powers of the chiefs in the basic Ordinance #30, 1913.

#7 (1919) Protectorate (Amendment) Ordinance.
Introduced a new office of Deputy Head Chief and refined method of appointing and removing Protectorate officials. Also introduced a new scale of yard taxes.

#13 (1944) Protectorate Courts Ordinance.
Repealed Ordinance #5, 1935, and instituted a High Court for the Protectorate with some power as the Supreme Court of the Colony. Continued a Protectorate Court in each Division. Established two classes of Magistrates.

#15 (1944) Protectorate (Amendment) Ordinance.
Changed title of certain territorial divisions and administrative areas. Added the position of Senior Commissioner.

#10 (1945) Native Authority (Amendment) Ordinance.
Gave Native Authorities the power to expel non-Gambians from the area of their jurisdiction.

#11 (1945) Protectorate (Amendment) Ordinance.
Amended Protectorate Ordinance #2, 1935, to allow fines imposed on Native Officials to be paid to the general revenue of the Native Authority.

#13 (1945) Protectorate Treasuries Ordinance.
Established Authority of Group Treasuries. Established a Finance committee to manage the Treasuries with a paid Treasury scribe. Established sources of revenue for such Treasuries, provided for budget estimates and better bookkeeping. Gave the authorities the right to impose, under certain conditions, local rates.

#16 (1945) Protectorate Land Ordinance.
Vested all Protectorate lands in the Authorities for each District. Established a land register and provided for leases to non-indigenes.

#13 (1946) Protectorate (Amendment) Ordinance.
Amended Ordinance #2, 1935, by removing British Kombo from the Protectorate system.

#16 (1946) Education Ordinance.
Section #13 gave the Native Authorities the right to open new schools under the general supervision of the Protectorate Education Officer.

#7 (1947) Protectorate (Amendment) Ordinance.
This brought Ordinance #3, 1933 and Ordinance #2, 1935 closer together by defining "Native Authority" in terms of the definition of 1933 and by substituting "Native Authority" for Chiefs in Section 13 of Ordinance of 1935.

#10 (1947) Protectorate Treasuries (Validation) Ordinance.
No Proclamation was ever issued putting Ordinance #13, 1945 into effect. Since Treasuries had been established, it was necessary to enact this ordinance making such establishments legal.

POLITICAL: LAW

Ewart, Frederick K. Notes on the Trial and Treatment of Juvenile Offenders (1944).

Gray, Sir John. Notes on Criminal Procedure in Subordinate Courts (1934).

_____, comp. A Revised Edition of the Ordinances of the Colony
  of the Gambia (1942).

Hopkinson, Dr. E. Notes on the Laws of the Gambia Protectorate
  1885-1923 (1926).

Kingdon, Donald, comp. A Chronological Table and an Index of
  the Ordinances of the Colony of the Gambia, 1901-1908 (London:
  1909).

Montagu, Algernon, and Francis Smith, comps. Ordinances of the
  Settlement on the Gambia, Passed in the Years Between the 10th
  August 1818 and 30 December 1885, 3 vols. (London: 1882-87).

Russell, Alexander, comp. Ordinances of the Colony of the Gambia
  in Force 31 July 1900, with an Appendix Containing Rules under
  Ordinances, 2 vols. (London: 1900).

Thompson, J. H., and Donald Kingdon, comps. The laws of the
  Gambia in Force on the 1st day of January 1955, 6 vols. (London: 1955).

POLITICAL: POLITICAL PARTIES

"P. S. N'Jie," Portrait, West Africa, 3 May 1958, p. 411.

"Training period for Gambian Politicians," New Commonwealth,
  June 1959, p. 410.

"Politics in the Gambia," West Africa, 21 May 1960, p. 563.

"General Election in the Gambia," New Commonwealth, Sept. 1960,
  p. 468.

"One Gambia Party Now Seeks Independence," New Commonwealth,
  Sept. 1960, p. 606.

"Gambia has a Chief Minister," New Commonwealth, May 1961, p. 328.

"Man of the People," Portrait (P. S. N'Jie), West Africa, 29 July
  1961, p. 823.

"Campaigning in the Gambia," West Africa, 19 May 1962, p. 535.

"New Men in the Gambia," West Africa, 9 June 1962, p. 619.

"The Gambia--May Elections," West Africa, 23 April 1966, p. 463.

"Jawara Wins Again," West Africa, 14 April 1972.

"Gambia Election Report," West Africa, 18 April 1977.

"Democracy at Work," West Africa, 15 May 1978.

Manjang, Ousman. "The Gambian General Elections," West Africa, 10 May 1982, pp. 1241-1242.

_____. "Gambian Liberation," West Africa, 26 July 1982, pp. 1929-1931.

POLITICAL: FOREIGN AFFAIRS

GREAT BRITAIN, PAPERS BY COMMAND

"Correspondence Respecting the Affairs of the Gambia and the Proposed Exchange with France," Cmnd. 1409 (1876).

"Petitions from the Inhabitants of the Gambia," Cmnd. 1498 (1876).

ARTICLES

"Gambia and Senegal Get Together," New Commonwealth, June 1961, p. 393.

"The Gambia and the OAU," West Africa, 5 June 1965, p. 618.

"Gambia Feels Pressure from Senegal," New Commonwealth, Nov. 1960, p. 739.

"Gambia's Links with Her Neighbours," New Commonwealth, Jan. 1960, p. 57.

"The Smuggling Problem," West Africa, 12 and 19 April, 1969.

Bentsi-Enchill, Nii K. "Year of Confederation," West Africa, 10 January 1983, pp. 69-70.

_____. "Senegambia: Implementation Stage," West Africa, 9 August 1982, pp. 2047-2049.

_____. "Senegambia Notebook," pt. 1, West Africa, 8 February 1982, pp. 353-355; pt. 2, 15 February 1982, pp. 423-426.

_____. "Sir Dawda Explains the Confederation," West Africa, 18 January 1982, pp. 137-141.

_____. "Senegalese Presence in the Gambia," West Africa, 11 January 1982, pp. 78-81.

Gaye, Babouar. "Killing Two Birds with One Stone," West Africa, 9 Sept. 1985, pp. 1864-1865.

Harrison-Church, R. J. "Gambia and Senegal: Senegambia," Geography Magazine, Sept. 1966, pp. 339-350.

Hatton, P. H. S. "The Gambia, the Colonial Office and the Opening Months of the First World War," Journal of African History, Vol. 7, No. 1, 1966, pp. 123-132.

Robson, P. "Problem of Senegambia," Journal of Modern African Studies, Oct. 1965, pp. 393-407.

Sey, Fatou. "Living with the ERP," West Africa, 20 Oct. 1986, pp. 2208-2209.

Welch, Claude E., Jr. "Gambia and the U.N. Report," West Africa, 4 July 1964, p. 741.

_____. "Is Senegambia Any Closer," West Africa, Part I, 7 March 1964, p. 263; Part II, 14 March 1964, p. 285; Part III, 21 March 1964, p. 313.

SCIENTIFIC: GEOGRAPHY

BOOKS

Dallimore, H. A Geography of West Africa (United Society for Christian Literature: 1948). See pp. 17-23 for the Gambia.

Jarrett, H. Reginald. A Geography of Sierra Leone and the Gambia (London: 1954). Jarrett was stationed in the Gambia during World War II. This book is an outgrowth of his personal observations and research for the M.A. and Ph.D. from London University. Although very basic, it is the only published geographical text on the Gambia.

Lucas, C. P. A Historical Geography of the British Colonies (London: 1894). See Vol. III for the Gambia.

Reed, F. R. C. The Geology of the British Empire (London: 1949). A brief discussion of the Gambia is on pp. 218-219.

ARTICLES

Gordon, E.   "A Land-Use Map of Kuntaur in the Gambia," Geographical Journal, Vol. 116, Nos. 4-6, 1950, pp. 216-217.

Jarrett, H. R.   "Major Natural Regions of the Gambia," Scottish Geographical Magazine, Dec. 1949, pp. 140-144.

_____.   "Geographical Regions of the Gambia," Scottish Geographical Magazine, Dec. 1950, pp. 163-169.

_____.   "Bathurst: Port of the Gambia River," Geography, May 1951, pp. 98-107.

Teague, Michael.   "The Gambia," Geographical Magazine, Nov. 1961, pp. 380-392.

SCIENTIFIC: GEOLOGY

Cooper, W. G. G.   "Report of a Rapid Geological Survey of the Gambia, British West Africa," Gold Coast Geological Survey Bulletin, No. 3, 1927.

Webb, Dr. R. A.   Report on Soil Research, May 1952-May 1954 (Bathurst: 1955).

"Gambia's Mineral Development," West Africa, 21 Aug. 1954, p. 785.

"Ilmenite Agreement," New Commonwealth, Sept. 1954, p. 263.

SCIENTIFIC: MEDICINE

Gamble, D. P.   "Infant Mortality Rates in Rural Areas in the Gambia Protectorate," Journal of Tropical Medicine and Hygiene, July 1952, pp. 145-149.

Haslett, A. W.   "West Africa Experiment" (on standard of living at Genieri), Penguin Science News, No. 23, 1952, pp. 108-113.

Horn, D. W.   "Infant Mortality in Bathurst," Gambia Annual Medical and Sanitary Report, 1942, pp. 12-14.

Hutchinson, M. P.   "The Epidemiology of Human Trypanosomiasis in British West Africa," Annual of Tropical Medicine and Parasitology, No. 47, 1953, pp. 156-158.

Jones, C. R. "Report on the Medical and Health Services of the Gambia," Gambia Government, Sessional Paper #2 (1970).

McCullough, F. S., and B. O. L. Duke. "Observations on the Potential Snail Vectors of Schistosoma Haematobium and S. Mansoni," Annual of Tropical Medicine and Parasitology, #48, 1954, pp. 277-286.

McFadzean, J. A., and J. F. McCourt. "Leprosy in Gambia, West Africa," Leprosy Review, Vol. 26, No. 2, April 1955, pp. 57-64.

McFadzean, J. A., and R. A. Webb. "Trace Element Deficiencies in Gambia," Transactions of Royal Society of Tropical Medicine and Hygiene, No. 51, 1957, pp. 425-428.

McGregor, I. A., and D. A. Smith. "A Health, Nutrition, and Parasitological Survey in a Rural Village (Keneba) in West Kiang, Gambia," Transactions of Royal Society of Tropical Medicine and Hygiene, Vol. 46, No. 4, 1952, pp. 403-427.

Savery, G. "The Gambia's War on Disease," West African Review, May 1956, pp. 489-493.

SCIENTIFIC: NATURAL SCIENCE

Hopkinson, Dr. E. "Birds of the Gambia," Elder Dempster Magazine, Jan. 1929, Vol. 7, pp. 129-132.

_____. "The Ducks of the Gambia," Journal of the Royal African Society, XXXV. Jan. 1936, pp. 48-52.

Johnson, E. "List of Vanishing Gambian Mammals," Journal of the Society for the Preservation of the Fauna of the Empire. Part 21. May 1937, pp. 62-66.

Clarke, J. R. "The Hippopotamus in Gambia, West Africa," Journal of Mammalogy, Vol. 34, No. 3, August 1053, pp. 294-315.

SOCIAL: ANTHROPOLOGY AND ARCHAEOLOGY

BOOKS

Gamble, David P. The Wolof of the Senegambia (London: 1957). Gamble undoubtedly knows more of the Gambia than any other person. He spent years in the Gambia, living and working in close proximity with the native people. He speaks Mandinka and Wolof and has written on a variety of subjects concerned with the area. This book is a revision of his doctoral disseration and represents more than five years' work. It is concise, informative, and the only good anthropological study of any of the five major peoples living in the Gambia.

Haddon, A. C. Wandering of Peoples (London: 1911).

ARTICLES

Ames, David. "The Dual Function of the 'Little People' of the Forest in the Lives of the Wolof," Journal of American Folklore, Jan.-March 1958.

_____. "The Economic Base of Wolof Polygamy," Southwestern Journal of Anthropology, Winter 1955.

_____. "The Selection of Mates: Courtship and Marriage Among the Wolof," Bulletin de l'Institut Français d'Afrique Noire, No. 1-2, 1956.

_____. "The Use of a Transitional Cloth-Money Token Among the Wolof," American Anthropologist, Oct. 1955.

_____. "Belief in Witches Among the Rural Wolof of the Gambia," Africa, Journal of the International African Institute, July 1959.

Beale, P. O. "The Stone Circles of the Gambia and the Senegal," Tarikh, Vol. 2, No. 2, 1968, p. 1.

Beale, P. O., and F. A. Evans. The Anglo-Gambian Stone Circles Expedition, 1964-65, A Report (Bathurst: 1966).

Parker, Harry. "Stone Circles in the Gambia," Journal of the Royal Anthropological Institute, Vol. 53, Jan.-June 1923.

Southorn, Lady Bella. "Mysterious stone circles of the Gambia," Crown Colonist, 1938, pp. 309-310. An account of a visit to a circle at Niani Maru.

Weil, Peter M. "Language Distribution in the Gambia 1966-67," African Language Review #7, 1968, pp. 101-106.

_____. "Mandinka Mansaya: The Role of the Mandinka in the Political System of the Gambia." Ann Arbor: University Microfilms, 1968.

SOCIAL: DEMOGRAPHY

Jarrett, H. R. "Population and Settlement in the Gambia," Geographic Review, Oct. 1948, pp. 633-636.

GAMBIA GOVERNMENT, SPECIALIZED
REPORTS

"Report of the Census Commissioner for Bathurst, 1944," Sessional Paper #2 (1945).

"Report of the Census Commissioner for the Colony, 1951," Sessional Paper #4 (1952).

"Report on the Census of the Population of the Gambia, April 1963," Sessional Paper #13 (1965).

SOCIAL: EDUCATION

GAMBIA GOVERNMENT, SPECIALIZED
REPORTS

Allen, R. C. Education in the Gambia: Present Organisation and Possible Future Development (1939).

Baldwin, T. H. "Report of Commissioner Appointed to Make Recommendations on ... Education in Gambia," Sessional Paper #7 (1951).

Gwilliam, (Miss). Report on the training of teachers and ways of improving Primary education by the Assistant Education Advisor to the Secretary of State (1953).

McMath, Dr. A. M. "Report on Infant and Girls Education," Sessional Paper #4 (1943).

Weston, H. C., and F. J. Harlow. Survey of technical and further education, Sierra Leone and Gambia (1949).

Education Department. Annual Report. (Issued as Sessional Papers of the Legislative Council.)

"Secretary of State Decisions on Dr. McMath's Short Term for the Development of Education in Bathurst," Sessional Paper #9 (1944).

"Conclusions Reached subsequent to S. P. #9/44 on Short Term Proposals for Development of Education in Bathurst," Sessional Paper #4 (1945).

"Scholarships and Financial Assistance toward the Attainment of Higher Education Qualifications," Sessional Paper #6 (1946).

"Education Policy of the Gambian Government, 1961-65," Sessional Paper #1 (1965).

SOCIAL: RELIGION

Anderson, J. N. D. Islamic Law in Africa (London: 1954). See pp. 225-248 for the Gambia.

Daly, T. C. S. "The Problem of a Young Diocese," East and West Review, July 1948, pp. 72-75.

Fisher, Humphrey. "Ahmadiyya in the Gambia, French Territories and Liberia," West Africa, 27 January 1962, p. 93.

Haythornthwaite, W. "The Church in the Gambia," East and West Review, Vol. 14, 1950, pp. 122-125.

SOCIAL: SOCIOLOGY

Forde, C. D. Report on the Need for Ethnographic and Sociological Research in the Gambia (1945).

Jarrett, H. R. "The Strange Farmers of the Gambia," Geographical Review, Oct. 1949, pp. 649-657.

Jectson, Seth. "Njuli Boys: Circumcision Rites in the Gambia," West African Review, Oct. 1952, p. 1035.

Rees, J. G. "Housing in a Gambian Village," African Affairs, July 1952, pp. 230-237.

Southorn, Lady Bella. "The Old Woman of Fattato," West African Review, July 1938, pp. 17-18.

Weil, Peter M. "Tradition and Opposition in Area Council Elections in the Gambia," Journal of Asian and African Studies, April 1971, pp. 108-117.